135789

D1340129

The Differentiated Flipped Classroom

For our families, friends, colleagues, teachers, and students

The Differentiated Flipped Classroom

A Practical Guide to Digital Learning

Eric M. Carbaugh

Kristina J. Doubet

Foreword by Carol Ann Tomlinson

CORWIN
A SAGE Company

FOR INFORMATION:

Corwin
A SAGE Company
2455 Teller Road
Thousand Oaks, California 91320
(800) 233-9936
www.corwin.com

SAGE Publications Ltd.
1 Oliver's Yard
55 City Road
London EC1Y 1SP
United Kingdom

SAGE Publications India Pvt. Ltd.
B 1/I 1 Mohan Cooperative Industrial Area
Mathura Road, New Delhi 110 044
India

SAGE Publications Asia-Pacific Pte. Ltd.
3 Church Street
#10-04 Samsung Hub
Singapore 049483

Executive Editor: Arnis Burvikovs
Associate Editor: Ariel Price
Editorial Assistant: Andrew Olson
Production Editor: Melanie Birdsall
Copy Editor: Deanna Noga
Typesetter: C&M Digitals (P) Ltd.
Proofreader: Caryne Brown
Indexer: Molly Hall
Cover Designer: Janet Kiesel
Marketing Manager: Maura Sullivan

Copyright © 2016 by Corwin

All rights reserved. When forms and sample documents are included, their use is authorized only by educators, local school sites, and/or noncommercial or nonprofit entities that have purchased the book. Except for that usage, no part of this book may be reproduced or utilized in any form or by any means, electronic or mechanical, including photocopying, recording, or by any information storage and retrieval system, without permission in writing from the publisher.

All trademarks depicted within this book, including trademarks appearing as part of a screenshot, figure, or other image, are included solely for the purpose of illustration and are the property of their respective holders. The use of the trademarks in no way indicates any relationship with, or endorsement by, the holders of said trademarks.

Printed in the United States of America

Library of Congress Cataloging-in-Publication Data

Carbaugh, Eric M.

The differentiated flipped classroom: A practical guide to digital learning / Eric M. Carbaugh, Kristina J. Doubet; foreword by Carol Ann Tomlinson.

pages cm
Includes bibliographical references and index.

ISBN 978-1-5063-0296-6 (pbk. : alk. paper)

1. Video tapes in education. 2. Individualized instruction. 3. Homework. I. Doubet, Kristina. II. Title.

LB1044.75.C37 2015
371.39'4—dc23   2015027879

This book is printed on acid-free paper.

ST. HELENS
COLLEGE

371·394
CAR

135789

Oct 2016

LIBRARY

Certified Chain of Custody
SUSTAINABLE
FORESTRY
INITIATIVE
Promoting Sustainable Forestry
www.sfiprogram.org
SFI-01268
SFI label applies to text stock

15 16 17 18 19 10 9 8 7 6 5 4 3 2 1

DISCLAIMER: This book may direct you to access third-party content via web links, QR codes, or other scannable technologies, which are provided for your reference by the author(s). Corwin makes no guarantee that such third-party content will be available for your use and encourages you to review the terms and conditions of such third-party content. Corwin takes no responsibility and assumes no liability for your use of any third-party content, nor does Corwin approve, sponsor, endorse, verify, or certify such third-party content.

Contents

APPENDICES

List of Figures

Foreword

In the early stages of introducing technology into American classrooms (not very long ago, really, in the scheme of things), Apple donated computers to schools and classrooms to be used by teachers for the benefit their instruction and student learning. Because the computer company had ample resources, it sent "coaches" along with the computers to help teachers acclimate to the new technology. Again, because of adequate funding to support long-term work, the coaches remained in the schools, on and off, over a period of about 10 years. This arrangement had a two-pronged benefit. First, teachers in the selected schools had knowledgeable support in learning about computers. Second, the Apple coaches had time to understand what facilitated and impeded teacher use of computers for instructional purposes.

In regard to the latter, an interesting—and not very surprising—thing happened. Many teachers found the computers to be more of a hindrance than a blessing! Given a choice, they'd have put the computers back in their boxes—or at the very least, sent the coaches packing.

It turns out that technology was really neither the problem nor the solution to the problem. Learning to use computers was of scant value to the teachers until they began to reinvent their visions of teaching and learning. They needed to move from a teacher-centered to a student-centered view of the classroom, from teacher as teller to teacher as facilitator, from student as listener and absorber to student as collaborator and sometimes expert, from knowledge as accumulation to knowledge as transfer and transformation, from a learning emphasis on facts and replication to relationships and inquiry, from success defined quantitatively to success defined qualitatively, from assessment as testing to assessment as performance, and from instruction focused on seatwork to instruction focused on communication, collaboration, and expression.

On its face, that change is revolutionary. In reality, it was evolutionary. Teachers tended to progress through a series of "movements" over time. Early in the progression, they simply learned about the technology so that it seemed less intimidating. In time, they began to use the technology—often slowly—to support traditional instruction. Later, they used the computers to support student productivity in things like word processing and math practice—still in the context of traditional thinking and planning. Later still, the teachers began to envision and use computers as one tool available to students in doing interdisciplinary and project-based work. And finally, the teachers (or many of them, at least) began to use computers, in combination with many other tools, in innovative ways that served their own purposes and those of their students. The ACOT coaches as researches spoke of these developmental stages as resistance, adoption, adaptation, appropriation, and invention.

Along the way, the teachers began to trust that their students could learn when a teacher was not "standing over them." They also came to believe that learning was something that must happen *in* students, not *to* them. At the same time, the teachers began to conceive curriculum as a plan to engage students with critical ideas and skills rather than as a race to cover data, and they became facilitators and guides in that process rather than dispensers of facts.

At each juncture along the way, teachers and students were "freed up" to become more inquiry-oriented, more thoughtful, and more original. It was not uncommon for teacher and student to "reverse roles," with all classroom players learning from and teaching one another. As the transformation developed, the computers shifted from an annoyance that was imposed on teachers to a potential means for accomplishing valued ends.

Most really promising approaches to teaching and learning require that teachers embark on a journey—a transformation—very similar to the one the ACOT teachers encountered. It's almost never the strategy or the model or the innovation per se that's going to transform teaching and learning. What makes the difference is growth-oriented teachers who come to understand the essential nature of teaching and learning and who then realize the potential of a curricular model, instructional approach, or set of technologies to help them become authentic teachers and their students become authentic learners.

The ACOT journey—the transformation from resistance to adoption to adaption to appropriation to innovation—is a precursor to effective differentiation and to effective classroom flipping. On the one hand, flipping and differentiation seem like a dual transformation—twice the effort, twice the risk. In reality, however, the two approaches ask the same thing of teachers—an emphasis on student as meaning maker and teacher as guide and facilitator who has a willingness to innovate. Differentiation seeks one additional shift—acknowledging the reality that students rarely enter or exit a lesson at the same point and that, for many students, real learning can't happen until the teacher acts on that reality.

It is at this intersection that both flipping and differentiation become prime partners. Flipping exists to provide classroom time for a teacher to coach for student understanding rather than using class time largely or solely to dispense information. Differentiation provides a model that enables teachers to use that classroom time to attend to learner variance rather than working from the assumption that "batch instruction" is the best we can do.

In this book, the authors provide a frame for understanding the power of combining flipping and differentiation, and they present the two approaches not as add-ons to teaching, but rather as core to achieving what the vast majority of teachers aspire to achieve—significant and observable growth for every student who comes their way. The book clearly presents the underpinnings of effective instruction, embeds their guidance flipping and differentiation solidly in those underpinnings, and provides sound instructional strategies for attending to student learning differences in the context of a flipped classroom. In essence, they present Ms. Velazquez's ACOT transformation as a metaphor for the kind of change that's critically needed in today's classrooms so that they can become contemporary places of learning for today's students.

Edward Land, inventor of Polaroid, commented that change is the mandate of nature as we can observe it on every hand. Today's successes, he cautioned, become tomorrow's failures. Not to grow is to die.

The irony, of course, is that he seems to have overlooked his own advice. So successful was Polaroid—so up-to-date or even ahead of the game—that it seemed unnecessary to push the margins of change. He gave us, for a brief time, a great camera system—and then another example of today's successes becoming tomorrow's failures.

Most of us as teachers work very hard. Most of us see ourselves as successful. This book challenges us to grow anyway. It's the right challenge at the right time for the right reasons.

—Carol Ann Tomlinson, EdD

William Clay Parrish, Jr., Professor and Chair
Educational Leadership, Foundations, and Policy
Curry School of Education
University of Virginia

Acknowledgments

We could not have written this book without the support and collaboration of many people who are important to both our personal and professional lives.

We are grateful to Ed Milliken, who planted the seeds of inspiration that grew into this book.

The tireless efforts of Stephen Caviness and Gabrielle Munns, our graduate assistants, made this book possible. They created meaningful examples, provided vital fact-checking and alignment skills, and encouraged us every day with their enthusiasm and dedication. We are grateful.

To our James Madison University College of Education students: Your commitment to your calling and your diligence in seeking excellence fills us with hope for the future of education in this country and beyond.

A huge "thank you" to the classroom teachers and administrators across the country with whom we have the privilege to work alongside. We learn from you daily, and we applaud you for your tireless investment in your students.

To those who provided invaluable feedback on the manuscript at various points in the process—we appreciate your questions, insights, and suggestions. Thank you for making us sharper!

We are filled with gratitude for our mentors, colleagues, and friends:

> Carol Tomlinson, our advisor and teacher—we will never cease to be inspired by your expertise and your example.

> Steve Purcell, our department chair and model for humility in leadership—we thank you for your unwavering support.

> Jessica Hockett and Marcia Imbeau, our friends and colleagues—thank you for your feedback, discernment, and encouragement.

To Arnis Burvikovs, Ariel Price, Andrew Olson, Melanie Birdsall, Deanna Noga, and everyone else in the Corwin family—thank you for this opportunity, for making us feel welcome, and for your support throughout this process.

Finally and most importantly, we offer our deepest appreciation to our families for their steadfast love, support, psychotherapy, and encouragement. Thank you for being our biggest fans, even when we don't deserve it.

PUBLISHER'S ACKNOWLEDGMENTS

Corwin gratefully acknowledges the following reviewers for their editorial insight and guidance:

Debbie Alexander-Davis, Faculty
    and Residency Supervisor
Tennessee Technological University
Cookeville, TN

William Chamberlain, Teacher
McDonald County R-1 School
    District
Anderson, MO

Garrett Eastman, Director of Libraries
Becker College
Worcester, MA

Jason Ellingson, Superintendent
Collins-Maxwell CSD
Ames, IA

Daniel Elliott, Professor,
    Professional Education
William Jessup University
Rocklin, CA

Nancy Foote, National Board
    Certified Teacher
Higley Unified School District
Queen Creek, AZ

Tara Fortner, Assistant Professor
    of Education
Lyndon State College
Lyndonville, VT

Dr. Jessica Hockett,
    Educational Consultant
Jessica A. Hockett, Inc.
Evanston, IL

Chris Hubbuch, Principal
Excelsior Springs Middle School
Excelsior Springs, MO

Kathryn McCormick,
    Math Teacher
Gahanna Middle School East
Gahanna, OH

Nishant N. Mehta,
    Head of School
The Children's School
Atlanta, GA

Drew Miller, Head Principal
Montevideo Middle School
Penn Laird, VA

Sandra Moore, English
   Language Arts Teacher
Coupeville High School
Coupeville, WA

Jen Pease, Adjunct Instructor
   of Teacher Education
University of Virginia
Charlottesville, VA

John Robinson, Principal/Teacher
Newton Conover City Schools
Newton, NC

Dr. Jennie Snyder, Superintendent
Piner-Olivet Union School District
Santa Rosa, CA

Nancy White, 21st Century
   Learning and Innovation Specialist
Academy School District
Colorado Springs, CO

About the Authors

 **Eric M. Carbaugh, PhD,** is an Associate Professor in the Department of Middle, Secondary, and Mathematics Education at James Madison University, where he has received the College of Education's "Distinguished Service Award" and been twice nominated for the College's "Distinguished Teacher Award." Eric is an international education consultant as well ASCD Faculty member. To date, he has worked with over 65 schools and districts on differentiated instruction, the *Understanding by Design* curriculum framework, quality formative and summative assessment design, and other various educational best practices. Eric has authored numerous articles and book chapters and is also journal editor and board member for the Virginia ASCD chapter. Eric taught secondary school social studies as well as elementary language arts and history. He currently lives outside Charlottesville, Virginia, and can be reached at carbauem@jmu.edu.

 **Kristina J. Doubet, PhD,** is an Associate Professor in the Department of Middle, Secondary, and Mathematics Education at James Madison University, where she has received the College of Education's "Distinguished Teacher Award" and "Madison Scholar Award." As a consultant and ASCD Faculty Member, Kristi has partnered with over 80 schools, districts, and organizations—both nationally and abroad—around initiatives related to differentiated instruction, *Understanding by Design*, and classroom assessment. In addition to numerous journal articles and book chapters, she coauthored the AMLE book *Smart in the Middle: Classrooms That Work for Bright Middle-Schoolers* (with Carol Tomlinson) and the ASCD book *Differentiation in Middle and High School: Strategies to Engage ALL Learners* (with Jessica Hockett). Kristi taught secondary English and language arts for 10 years and has also served as an instructional coach in elementary and middle school classrooms. She can be reached at doubetkj@jmu.edu.

Preface

Attention is not in itself such an automatic process as you might presume. To make it work, it has to be activated, and if not, the opportunity to learn slips past.

—Hattie & Yates, 2014

A 1999 study conducted by Christopher Chabris and Daniel Simons, and replicated numerous times since, asked college students to watch a video for 75 seconds and count the number of times the individuals on the screen passed around a basketball. About halfway through the video, either a woman with an umbrella or a person dressed in a gorilla costume walked across the screen in the middle of the action for about 5 seconds. After watching the video, participants were questioned about what they had observed in the video. Almost half—46% to be exact—did not report seeing the unexpected event to which they were exposed.

You may be asking yourself: "How could anyone miss a gorilla walking across the screen? Or a woman with an umbrella in the middle of a basketball exercise?" Although it seems unlikely, these findings clearly illustrate that not everyone walks away with the same experience after viewing a video—or any other kind of learning, for that matter. When asked to focus intently on something, our brains may miss events that unfold right in front of our eyes; alternately, we may become distracted by events happening on the periphery.

Let's revisit this example from a different perspective—that of what we would like students to learn when asking them to view recorded content at home. If the video in the Chabris and Simmons (1999) experiment was designed as a flipped learning tool, then the teacher's goal might be that students *will be able to correctly identify the number of times a ball was passed*. However, the teacher may have failed to consider the many factors that influence whether or not students would be able to focus on and process the video's content. What he or she may find is that roughly half of his or her students were able to hyper-focus and achieve the learning goal, while the other half were distracted by other extraneous factors or even by their readiness to engage with the material. If the teacher assumed he or she would be starting with everyone on the same page the next day, he or she would be wrong.

The point is this: Teachers need to take active measures to guide student focus and attention to specific learning goals, particularly when students are acquiring content outside of school. And they need to account for the differences that will inevitably emerge regarding how students process such a learning experience. Educators cannot guarantee student attention and progress, but they can create favorable conditions to facilitate them. This book explores many ways to achieve these goals, embracing the principles of a differentiated classroom to make flipping more effective both at home and at school.

THE FLIPPED INSTRUCTIONAL MODEL

A steadily increasing number of classrooms are moving to the Flipped model of instruction, using educational technology to present new material to students at home and utilizing class time to review, reinforce, and practice. In fact, between 2012 and 2014 alone, the number of teachers who reported flipping a lesson grew from 48% to 78% (Yarbro, Arfstrom, McKnight, & McKnight, 2014). During this same time period (2013–2014), financing for education technology companies rose 55% (Singer, 2015), suggesting an interaction between a greater number of resources and more teachers willing to utilize them through flipped instruction. As more and more teachers buy into the idea of flipping their classroom, attention is turning to what happens, pedagogically, *within* the flipped setup. In 2014, the Flipped Learning Network (FLN) established 11 indicators for educators to use to self-assess their flipped learning efforts or progress. These indicators include markers such as:

- F.2—I provide students with different ways to learn content and demonstrate mastery.

- L.1—I give students opportunities to engage in meaningful activities without the teacher being central.

- I.3—I differentiate to make content accessible and relevant to all students.

- P.2—I conduct ongoing formative assessments during class time through observation and by recording data to inform future instruction. (Yarbro et al., 2014, p. 6)

This book is intended to provide guidance in how to implement researched best educational practices—such as those bulleted above—within the Flipped model and through the lens of **differentiated instruction**—an instructional approach that allows teachers to address patterns in student learning by providing different methods of taking in, processing, and demonstrating learning with the goal of moving every student forward (Tomlinson, 2003; 2014). There is a logical synergy between these two models—the flipped environment provides rich opportunities to cater to diversity because of the flexibility linked to its use.

> This book isn't about simply *assuming* differentiation is happening through flipped instruction, but rather *ensuring* it happens.

Within these pages you will find an array of ideas to identify and address the various learning needs of students within a flipped environment. As Hattie (2012) notes: "The key is for teachers to have a clear reason for differentiation, and then relate what they do *differently* to where the student is located on the progression from novice to capable, relative to the learning intentions and success criteria" (p. 98). This book isn't about simply *assuming* differentiation is happening through flipped instruction, but rather *ensuring* it happens through purposeful, carefully planned **at-home** and **at-school** learning experiences, all while checking for student understanding.

One misconception that often accompanies a move to digital learning is the assumption that because students are online, they are learning. This is a dangerous assumption. In *any* environment—face-to-face or digital—we cannot simply hope that students are processing and reflecting on the content; rather, we must guide them to do so. As Hattie and Yates (2014) note: "Within the world of psychology, there is no thing such as passive learning, unless the term implies learning to do nothing, in a manner akin to learned helplessness" (p. 47). An instructional strategy is only as good as the impact it has on student learning.

This book, therefore, is designed to function as a guide to creating Flipped Learning experiences that actively engage *all* students on a more appropriate level—embracing technology as a tool to do so both at home and at school.

PURPOSE AND USE OF THIS BOOK

This book is structured to practically guide teachers in Grades 5 through 12 through the process of differentiating their flipped classrooms. Although the examples we provide are geared more toward middle and high school standards and curricula, the principles, tools, and strategies we include are suitable for students of any age who are tech-savvy in both at-home and at-school settings.

The strategies described herein are designed for educators who operate in a technology-rich environment (e.g., one-to-one initiatives, purposeful use of personal devices, access to school laptop and tablet carts). One concern that often arises is that of student access to devices and Internet at home. In fact, Project Tomorrow cites this issue as one of the primary hindrances for educators wishing to flip their classrooms (Yarbro et al., 2014). While there is no magic bullet to give every student access to the same at-home resources, there are active steps that teachers and administrators can take. Figure P.1 offers solutions for dealing with these issues so that all students can participate in the strategies outlined in this book.

The structure of the book lends itself to reading as a whole or to selecting the chapters that best fit the needs of individual teachers, coaches, or administrators as well as whole-school faculties or professional learning communities (PLCs). Specifically, the book presents the following tools, strategies, and principles with applications for both at-home and at-school implementation:

> **Chapter 1** provides an overview of both Flipped Learning and differentiated instruction with the goal of exploring natural points of overlap between the two models.

> **Chapter 2** details how to establish an effective learning environment—both face-to-face and digitally—as a necessary foundation for flipping and differentiating.

> **Chapter 3** outlines digital and face-to-face strategies for collecting ongoing formative assessment data in a flipped environment to determine student needs.

> **Chapter 4** provides guidance and examples on how teachers might use this formative assessment data to design appropriately challenging instruction for differing degrees of student readiness (both at home and at school).

> **Chapter 5** looks at how teachers can use the Flipped model to motivate students by differentiating for student interests and learning profiles.

> **Chapter 6** addresses the reality that classroom management takes on an entirely new dynamic with a flipped instructional approach. This chapter provides practical solutions for teachers to better manage the at-home and at-school learning environments.

> **Chapter 7** provides a concise summary of take-away ideas as well as guidance for how to get started flipping and differentiating instruction.

> The **Appendices** contain multiple resources—such as additional strategy examples, a storehouse of technology tools, sample lesson plans, and a student technology survey—to support individual teacher learning, PLC studies, and professional development workshops.

It is our hope that teachers, no matter where they are in their level of experience, will glean strategies and tools that will allow them to facilitate and monitor, rather than to hope and assume, that active learning is taking place for the entire range of students in our charge.

FIGURE P.1: "ACCESS" TROUBLE SPOTS AND POSSIBLE SOLUTIONS

Trouble Spot	Possible Solutions
Students don't have access to devices for watching videos or the Internet at home.	If students don't have computer access, some of the following ideas can help give them view to the at-home content. However, some of the online tools for processing and posting ideas would also need to be changed. • **Burn videos** onto DVDs. Most students, if they don't have computers or the Internet, have access to a DVD player at home and can view videos this way. • Discuss the possibility of students **checking out devices** from the school media center. • **Start an effort throughout the school or community** to obtain older smartphones, iPods, tablets, or MP4 players that could be distributed to students to watch at-home content. If students have computers or tablets but Internet access is keeping them from watching the videos: • Students can download and **save/capture the videos** to their devices while at school for viewing that night at home. • Provide students with **a USB flash drive** that contains the videos recorded. Students can plug these into their computers to access the videos. • Encourage students to visit local libraries or other businesses with **free Wi-Fi access** (or computer access). Teachers can reach out to their community to determine if any local businesses, shops, or restaurants might be willing to permit some students to use their Internet resources.
Students without Internet and/ or computers and need to complete at-home differentiated assignments.	• Ask students to keep a **handwritten journal** and type their responses and upload them to their blogs, discussion threads, and so on during class the next day. • Encourage students to **communicate with peers over the phone** (landline or other) while watching content. • Allow students to bring in their work on a **USB flash drive.** During a warm-up activity the following day, students can post their ideas and questions to their blogs, discussion threads, and so on. • Scout out **local libraries** that have computers for the public to use or local businesses that have free Wi-Fi access and encourage students to utilize those resources. • If there is access to a **scanner** at school, allow students to scan their handwritten journal and upload it as a file to their blogs or a discussion thread. Inexpensive apps are available to scan documents with your smartphone, and the quality is typically quite good.

CHAPTER 1

Flipping and Differentiating

Finding Common Ground

Ms. Velazquez was an "early adopter" of the Flipped model in her middle school. To her, it made a lot of sense to let students spend "homework time" introducing themselves to new math content via video. Students were more motivated to watch videos for homework than they were to complete practice problems; additionally, she enjoyed the extra time she gained in class to answer questions and supervise students as they practiced and extended what they'd learned at home. Her school's one-to-one initiative ensured that all students had access to a laptop at home; those who didn't have Internet quickly adapted by either downloading videos onto USB flash drives before they left for the day or by using their smartphones to access videos via a cellular network. Although she had started off using Khan Academy videos for online instruction, she quickly embraced Adobe's "Captivate" technology and began making her own screen capture videos. She liked that she could use that forum to personalize her instruction, and she knew most students were watching the homework videos because they would often mention her attempts at "math humor" and the way she incorporated student names into the math scenarios featured in her videos.

> Those who didn't have Internet quickly adapted by either downloading videos onto USB flash drives before they left for the day or by using their smartphones to access videos cellular network.

But not *all* students were watching. And even those who *were* watching often remembered her jokes more than they did the math. Ms. Velazquez knew that students could pause, rewind, and re-watch portions of the videos if they became "stuck," but she had no assurance they were doing so . . . or that it helped if they did. Furthermore, the increased flexibility she gained during class time by flipping was losing its power as she struggled to determine how best to build in accountability measures for "homework" and to adjust instruction for the varying needs of students who showed up in class each day with different questions, levels of understanding, and degrees of motivation. She often felt her students were disconnected—from her and from each other—and that instruction was, at times, disjointed. In short, the flexibility that had begun as a source of *inspiration* was slowly but surely turning into a source of *exasperation*.

FLEXIBILITY—BOTH A BLESSING AND A CURSE

Flexibility is generally considered to be an asset. When we are flexible with our travel plans, we may experience less stress. When an employer is flexible with how and when employees accrue required work hours, those employees experience more freedom. Likewise, if a teacher is flexible about the rate or manner through which a student masters established learning goals, students may experience more success. However—as is true in all three examples—being flexible means the person in charge relinquishes a bit of control over the process. John Bergman (2013) asserts that teachers who flip their classrooms yield some of that control to their *students* as they assume more responsibility for their own learning. But, as Ms. Velazquez found, that shift in responsibility often shines a spotlight on variance in student learning needs. This is good news if teachers are interested in moving all students forward; being aware of what students need to succeed is the first step in helping them achieve! But it does present new challenges, because teachers must be more proactive in their planning to make sure those differing needs are met. In other words, **flipping instruction** presents teachers with rich opportunities to **differentiate instruction**.

> Both flipped and differentiated classrooms require investment and proactive planning. Both models require employing a student-centered approach to instruction, and both models require shifts in paradigm and structure.

Both flipped and differentiated classrooms require investment and proactive planning. Both models require employing a student-centered approach to instruction, and both models require shifts in paradigm and structure. Fortunately, these shifts do not run counter to one another; in fact, flipping and differentiating a classroom are very complementary transformations. This book explores what is vital to each model and how teachers can use those models in concert to better meet the needs of all students.

OVERVIEW OF A FLIPPED CLASSROOM

A Flipped instructional model takes advantage of technology to promote a more flexible learning environment. Through the recording of direct instruction—traditionally utilized as an in-class tool—teachers using a Flipped model assign these materials for students to process at home. This facilitates a more learner-centered in-class experience (Bergman & Sams, 2012), while providing students with preinstructional experiences to better prepare them for at-school learning (Hattie & Yates, 2014). Teachers who flip a lesson can assign small group or individual activities in class, freeing up time to monitor student progress, check for understanding, and provide feedback and assistance when necessary. Essentially, the classroom experience becomes much more focused on student processing and the development of ideas, moving away from students as passive receivers of information.

> **Flipped Classroom:** "Basically, the concept of a flipped class is this: that which is traditionally done in class is now done at home, and that which is traditionally done as homework is now completed in class" (Bergmann & Sams, 2012, p. 13).

The Flipped model discussed in this book adheres closely to the Flipped Learning Network's 2014 definition of "Flipped Learning":

> A pedagogical approach in which direct instruction moves from the group learning space to the individual learning space, and the resulting group space is transformed into a dynamic, interactive learning environment where the educator guides students as they apply concepts and engage creatively in the subject matter. (Yarbro et al., 2014, p. 5)

We believe, however, that the quality of the learning experience is important regardless of the "geography" of where it occurs; therefore, we focus on how to create dynamic interactive learning experiences, both **at home** and **at school**. Our discussion of Flipped Learning capitalizes on what we know about student learning, in general, from recent brain research and couples this information with the importance of creating a responsive classroom. The intent is to expand the structure of traditional schooling and provide teachers with additional flexibility to better meet the needs of their students. It is our belief that the most effective teachers can use flipped instruction to flexibly and *proactively* respond to the needs of their students. Our goal is to show how full or partial classroom flipping can help make teachers more effective at meeting the diverse needs of students.

BRAIN RESEARCH AND THE FLIPPED CLASSROOM: IMPLICATIONS FOR PRACTICE

We now know a great deal about how the brain takes in, manages, and retains learning. Of pivotal importance is nature of the **knowledge, processing opportunities**, and **social context** afforded to students during their learning experiences (Bransford, Brown, & Cocking, 2000). Therefore, in a flipped classroom, teachers must be sure to pay particular attention to the following when designing tasks and assignments:

Knowledge

Our brains work best when finding patterns and identifying relationships. When learning something new, students need opportunities to connect it to prevailing structures or neural networks—to **"hang" new knowledge on the scaffolding of existing knowledge** (Hattie, 2012; Sousa & Tomlinson, 2011). Thus, any flipped classroom should facilitate the development of connections and relationships among the concepts being learned, while avoiding teaching the same concepts in isolation. Rote lectures—live or recorded—absent of connections to previously learned material or personal relevance will not capitalize on the neural growth and retention associated with more engaging learning.

Processing Opportunities

Time for reflection and practice are essential to move information into long-term memory storage (Sousa & Tomlinson, 2011). This is particularly important in a flipped classroom because, even if students are watching lectures, they should be focused on specific learning outcomes, actively processing and reflecting on the content being presented. Much as a classroom lecture should include instructional questions for students to pause and reflect on ideas being presented, so too should a flipped lecture. In other words, teachers must **provide the necessary time and structure** for students to actively process learning and avoid the assumption that students are engaged with and retaining material simply because they are "watching" it.

Community

Learning experiences are most powerful when they are implemented in collaboration with others in a safe, orderly, and flexible community of learners (National Institute of Health, 2005; Sousa & Tomlinson, 2011). In-class learning activities, therefore, should take advantage of opportunities for students to wrestle with content in the company of peers who can both support and challenge them. As Hattie and Yates (2014) note: "Schooling is an inherently social process, and the attitudes of peers exert a strong impact on the individual" (p. 4). With the addition of the "virtual environment," the flipped classroom provides two forums for such students to work together—at home and at school. In other words, through the use of technology, even at-home learning experiences can occur within a collaborative environment.

While these three principles provide a vital and defensible foundation for any flipped experience, they also reflect one of the greatest challenges facing teachers who are interested in flipping their classrooms: *how to "best utilize additional classroom time"* in a flipped setup. In fact, Project Tomorrow cites this concern as one of the biggest barriers to implementation (Yarbro et al., 2014, p. 15). How do teachers ensure that students are actively processing important contextualized concepts in a collaborative fashion? We believe the answer to this quandary lies in adopting the principles and practices of Differentiated Instruction.

> **Differentiation:** "[T]eachers in differentiated classrooms accept and act on the premise that they must be ready to engage students in instruction through different approaches to learning, by appealing to a range of interests, and by using varied rates of instruction along with varied degrees of complexity and differing support systems" (Tomlinson, 2014, pp. 3–4).

OVERVIEW OF A DIFFERENTIATED CLASSROOM

Like the teacher of a flipped classroom, the teacher of a *differentiated* classroom strives for more flexibility in instruction, recognizing that one size certainly does not fit all. The quest to know students—who they are, what they are passionate about, how they learn best—drives the teacher's instructional decision making about how different students will access and master these ideas. Teachers in differentiated classrooms persistently seek to discover learner needs, and then persistently seek to find ways to meet those needs by adjusting content (what students learn), process (how students learn), and product (how students demonstrate what they have learned) to match the unique needs of a diverse range of learners (Tomlinson, 2003).

Recognizing that it is impossible to plan separate lessons for up to 150 students a day, the teacher of a differentiated classroom strives to find *patterns* among learner needs and to address those patterns through effective feedback and tailored assignments. Said differently, in a differentiated classroom the teacher (a) establishes clearly defined, high-quality learning goals, (b) consistently seeks to examine each student's progress in relationship to those goals, and (c) uses that information to make instructional decisions that advance the entire range of learners toward growth (d) in the context of a supportive and efficient learning environment (Sousa & Tomlinson, 2011).

Personalization and Differentiation

Recently, confusion has arisen regarding the connection between *personalization* and *differentiation*. While the terms are not synonymous, there is much overlap. Personalized learning refers to tailoring instruction and materials to the preferences and interests of various learners (Basye, 2014); thus, it seeks the same goals and employs similar means as differentiation. The distinguishing factor is the use of technology in the process. In other words:

> Personalized learning is a 21st Century model for differentiated instruction that addresses Tomlinson and Allan's (2000) vision of addressing each student's readiness, interest, and learning profile through differentiation of content, process and product. Personalized learning is often conceived of as an instructional method that incorporates technology and the use of mobile devices to help all students achieve high levels of learning. (Grant & Bayse, 2014, p. 21)

Differentiation, therefore, is the model; personalization is the goal; and technology is a means of accomplishing that goal. Since "differentiation" serves as the umbrella term in this relationship, we use that term to encompass "personalization."

BRAIN RESEARCH AND THE DIFFERENTIATED CLASSROOM: WHY DIFFERENTIATION MATTERS

Differentiation is not just a "good idea" or a "side consideration"; rather, it reflects the central tenets of how people learn. The National Research Council's recommendations for effective teaching practices assert that learning should be knowledge-centered, assessment-centered, learning-centered, and community-centered (Bransford et al., 2000). These recommendations align squarely with the essence of differentiation:

> Differentiation is not just a "good idea" or a "side consideration"; rather, it reflects the central tenets of how people learn.

Knowledge-Centered

Students in a successfully differentiated class grapple with important ideas and engage in inquiry, problem solving, and critical thinking (Sousa & Tomlinson, 2011). Recognizing that it is difficult to differentiate a "laundry list" of standards or low-level learning goals in a meaningful fashion (Bransford et al., 2000), teachers who successfully differentiate instruction ask *all* students to stretch toward high learning goals, and then support or challenge students as necessary, striking the proper balance between conceptual understanding and automaticity (Hattie, 2012). Students in a differentiated classroom focus on the *why* and the *how* of what they are studying rather than simply on the *who*, *what*, or *where*. They seek to make meaningful connections between past and present learning, as well as between what they are studying and the world around them.

Assessment-Centered

The teacher of a differentiated classroom recognizes the necessity of collecting and responding to student learning in an ongoing fashion with the goal of using that information to correct misconceptions, identify room for growth, and make instructional decisions accordingly (Bransford et al., 2000; Tomlinson, 2003). Neuroscientist Judy Willis (2011) explains that the adolescent brain responds favorably to video games because those games recognize and address the brain's need for "incremental goal progress" information. In other words, a video game alerts players to their standing and gives them immediate opportunities to adjust their strategy. Likewise, the teacher of a differentiated classroom frequently collects information about how students are processing instruction to provide them with (1) timely feedback about their progress and (2) targeted practice to address their mistakes and grow in expertise. In an assessment-centered classroom, teachers come face-to-face with the reality that different students will require different feedback and practice; therefore, these teachers respond with different tasks focused on the unique needs—or patterns of needs—of the learners in their charge.

Learner-Centered

All learners bring with them a portfolio of attitudes, interests, predispositions, conceptions, and misconceptions of learning. To be effective, instruction must address each of these head-on. The need for *relevance* is paramount, and the successful teacher will seek ways to make learning relevant for the class in general and to find opportunities for individual students to pursue areas of intrigue and interest (Bransford et al., 2000; Sousa & Tomlinson, 2011). Of course, it is impossible for teachers to make learning relevant for students if they do not know those students; therefore, in a differentiated classroom, teachers take active steps to build relationships with students with the goal of finding ways to connect them with content in meaningful ways.

Community-Centered

In a differentiated classroom, getting to know students is only a first step; teachers also strive to forge connections among students and to foster a collaborative atmosphere. The ideal classroom environment is one in which students feel the freedom to explore, take risks, and make mistakes with the shared understanding that mistakes are a prerequisite for success. In a differentiated classroom, the environment must also celebrate *difference* as a necessary ingredient for rich learning experiences (Bransford et al., 2000; Hattie, 2012). The deliberate discussion and exploration of classroom norms and individual differences is a nonnegotiable element of successful classroom management (Sousa & Tomlinson, 2011).

DIFFERENTIATING AND FLIPPING: A HARMONIOUS MATCH

As you may have noticed, these four tenets—particularly *knowledge-centered, assessment-centered,* and *community-centered*—mirror the previously discussed three principles of effective Flipped Learning (*knowledge, processing opportunities,* and *community*). In fact, a great deal of overlap exists among the principles of differentiation and those of Flipped Learning, suggesting that the two models can interact in a mutually beneficial fashion. The flipped classroom offers a rich environment in which to actively cultivate differentiation; likewise, differentiation offers an instructional model that can help teachers take advantage of the increased flexibility that a flipped classroom provides. This book examines the overlap between differentiation and flipping from two perspectives—what happens at home, and what happens in school—with an eye toward providing teachers with strategies for proactively meeting student needs in both settings. We present techniques for gathering assessment information as well as strategies for responding to that data. We examine methods for connecting students with content to increase motivation and foster a sense of relevancy. And we consider the nuts and bolts of management in a differentiated, flipped environment that are necessary for all the other techniques to actually work! First of all, however, we lay the groundwork for *all* these strategies by examining proactive steps to establishing a learning environment that provides an atmosphere of safety, respect, and collaboration—a vital foundation for both flipping and differentiating.

> The flipped classroom offers a rich environment in which to actively cultivate differentiation; likewise, differentiation offers an instructional model that can help teachers take advantage of the increased flexibility that a flipped classroom provides.

CHAPTER 2

Crafting and Maintaining a Positive Learning Environment

Community and Mindset

Recently, Drew Storen, a relief pitcher for Major League Baseball's Washington Nationals, was interviewed about overcoming the biggest setback of his career. In a deciding Game 5 against the St. Louis Cardinals in the National League Divisional Series in 2012, Drew was called on to keep the Cardinals' bats at bay and preserve a dwindling lead. Drew failed epically, on one of sports' biggest stages, in front of a national audience. The following year, he wasn't the same pitcher. His confidence was shaken—he no longer trusted his ability and was afraid of making mistakes.

Midway through the season, Drew was sent down to the minor leagues in what many perceived as a fall from grace. Except it wasn't. In fact, it was the beginning of his ascension back to not only one of the best pitchers on his team, but also in the entire league. But how did it happen? As Drew explains it, he didn't learn to work *harder* in the minor leagues, he learned to work *better*. He was taught to focus his efforts on mental toughness—on persistence—in the face of adversity, to attack each batter with a plan, to trust the defense behind him. Hundreds of major league pitchers have experienced what Drew did, and many of them never made it back. It wasn't just talent that helped Drew become successful, it was persistence and fortitude. It was a *growth mindset*.

Drew's story models the idea that, to succeed in creating a differentiated flipped classroom, teachers must cultivate and maintain a community of learners with growth mindsets. Students must feel valued, both by the teacher and their peers, and show them respect in return. They should be encouraged to explore important ideas, take risks, and make errors with the shared understanding that mistakes are a prerequisite for success. Teachers from Madison County, Virginia, developed the following definition of *classroom community*: "An environment where students feel safe, secure, and comfortable to learn, where participation and contribution are expected from every student, and where students see their role/ importance in the classroom" (personal communication, June 22, 2007).

Classroom community is a necessary condition for the development of a growth mindset, or the belief that intelligence is malleable, and that with enough effort, most people can do most things. Extensive classroom research uncovered the value of teachers emphasizing the growth potential of intelligence (Dweck, 2006). Students with a growth mindset "don't necessarily believe that anyone can become an Einstein or a Mozart, but they do understand that even Einstein and Mozart had to put in years of effort to become who they were. When students believe that they can develop their intelligence, they focus on doing just that" (Dweck, 2007, p. 34). Students with a growth mindset—a healthy sense of self-efficacy—persist in the face of challenges because they trust their potential. Teachers should take great care that all interactions with students model this belief.

There is the temptation to regard the ideas of mindset and community as "nice to have" or the "icing on the cake." After all, there is so much to cover in a typical class. Who has time to build community and foster an environment of risk taking? In reality, however, research into how the brain learns reveals that community and mindset might be better classified as "vital to have" or "the cake" itself rather than the icing. Findings from neuroscience reveal the following as a necessary affective foundation for student learning to take place (Sousa & Tomlinson, 2011):

1. Caring relationships—teacher-to-student and student-to-student—within the classroom.

2. Student ownership over, and investment in, their education.

3. Active and open confrontation of the fear of failure, which is a major obstacle to learning.

4. Positive interactions between students and teacher and among students, which raises the frontal lobe's ability to support memory.

Such measures are not just environment-centered; they are learning-centered. In fact, a meta-analysis of educational research found that the student-teacher relationship is among the highest factors predicting student success. In other words, the way teachers interact with students—their attention to community and mindset—is an essential part of effective teaching (Hattie, 2012).

> A finding from the 2012 Program for International Student Assessment (PISA) cites evidence to support the value of self-efficacy: "Practice and hard work go a long way towards developing each student's potential, but students can only achieve at the highest levels when they believe that they are in control of their success and that they are capable of achieving at high levels" (Organisation for Economic Co-operation and Development, p. 21, 2012).

PRACTICAL STRATEGIES FOR PROMOTING A HEALTHY LEARNING ENVIRONMENT

Ms. Velazquez—the teacher we met at the outset of Chapter 1—began flipping her classroom without deliberately attending to mindset or community. Thus, she was experiencing some frustrations with her learning environment, such as students who

> There are some intentional, or "overt" ways to build community and a growth mindset, but also some more "covert" messages that are communicated by how the teacher designs instruction (Doubet & Hockett, 2015).

felt disconnected from one another—and from her—and learning experiences she perceived as disjointed. Although teachers like Ms. Velazquez might feel the need for community—and may even know that research on student learning stresses its importance—they may not know how to go about fostering it in the classroom.

There are not only some intentional, or "overt," ways to build community and a growth mindset, but also some more "covert" messages that are communicated by how the teacher designs instruction (Doubet & Hockett, 2015). We first look at several overt community and mindset-building strategies before examining some instructional decisions that can also foster these more covertly, both at home and at school.

OVERT AT-SCHOOL METHODS FOR BUILDING COMMUNITY AND A GROWTH MINDSET COMMUNITY

Attendance Questions

To implement this community-building strategy, teachers pose questions at the beginning of class (to occasionally take the place of warm-up or bell-ringer questions) that are designed to elicit student opinions about various topics (Tomlinson & Doubet, 2005). For instance, a social studies teacher might start class by asking students what their favorite historical era is, or, completely unrelated to history, what the last song they listened to was. There are no wrong answers, and students who might be reluctant to participate in class discussions because of a perceived lack of content knowledge can certainly offer their responses. The benefits of Attendance Questions are not only that every student has a chance to get a "correct" answer, but also to provide them with opportunities to connect with other learners around the room. For instance, two students who are unfamiliar with each other might connect over the new Taylor Swift album they listened to or their love for Greek mythology as a historical topic.

Although Attendance Questions are primarily an at-school strategy, they can also be used at home to serve as the perfect warm-up for discussion board posts, back-channel tweets, and padlet.com responses. Before we ask students to respond to *academic* content in these online forums, it is a good idea to introduce those forums in *content-free* ways. This helps (1) ensure that everyone is familiar with the technology in a low-stakes manner and (2) begin to build bridges between students, even in our online learning space. Attendance Questions such as "Best Halloween costume ever?" or "If you could have any superpower, what would it be?" can get students used to interacting with and finding connections among one another in respectful ways, even from "behind their screens."

Different Shoes, Different Learning

Physical differences among students are visually apparent, but often their learning differences are less obvious. When we work with teachers in the field, there are always questions about students feeling less adequate if given different readiness tasks. One solution to this is the use of Flexible Grouping (discussed below as well as in Chapter 5), but another is acknowledging and communicating to students that they have different strengths, needs, interests, and learning preferences—and that to help create the most effective learning environment for them, students will sometimes be working on different activities, processing different content, and submitting different products.

To make this rationale clear to students, teachers might employ an activity that uses physical differences—in this case shoe size—to highlight learning differences. All students are asked to take off one shoe and put it in a pile at the front of the class. Students are then prompted to partner up and close their eyes while they are led by their partner to the shoe pile to blindly select a shoe. The students then switch roles so that both choose a shoe without seeing what they are selecting. This process continues until everyone in the class has some else's shoe. Students are then asked to stand in a circle and attempt to put on the shoe they have selected. Comic relief comes in the form of students in what look like clown shoes, or some that can barely fit their toes in the shoe. A discussion about variance in shoe size leads into dialogue about variance in learning, and that we cannot assume they have the same learning needs any more than we can assume they wear the same shoe size. Teachers might also pose questions to probe students' thoughts on mindset, like "Were your shoes always this size? Do you think your feet will continue to grow?" The point of this exercise is to encourage students to see differences as natural and to expect their teacher to embrace and plan for these differences with a belief in the growth potential of all students.

"ME" Postcards

This is a practice that we formerly used in our middle school classrooms and have translated into use with our preservice teachers as an introductory activity. At school, students fill in large note cards with images, drawn or pasted (physically or digitally), that represent who they are as individuals. Students can do this at home as well by utilizing simple technology such as PowerPoint. Images selected often include students' interests, affiliations, backgrounds, and even life hardships. Students explain the significance of each image on the back (or additional slide) and also take a brief moment to share these with the class. Teachers might even choose to display these in the room. Anecdotally, we can say with assurance that it is one of our favorite class days each semester, not only because we get to learn more about our students, but because we also get to see all the unintended connections students make with one another over shared experiences and interests. Last year, two students both realized their mothers were breast cancer survivors, and the year before that several students discovered a shared love for the *Wizarding World of Harry Potter* at Universal Orlando Resort. Just this past semester two students became fast friends bonding over the final episode of *How I Met Your Mother*. It is these relationships—teacher-to-student and student-to-student—that form a foundation for learning in any successful classroom. Figure 2.1 shows two examples from our students. They used a combination of digital and print technology to create these postcards.

MINDSET

With regard to helping foster a growth mindset at school, teachers can devote some class time to talking with students about their brains and how they all have the potential to improve. A 2007 study of adolescent learners found that if teachers can place emphasis on the potential of students—rather than the noticeable differences that might currently exist—there can be myriad motivational benefits for students (Blackwell, Trzesniewski, & Dweck, 2007). One example of how teachers might achieve this is for students to keep track of daily or weekly achievements that they once thought might be out of their reach. A two-sided journal illustrated in Figure 2.2, on page 16, might be used to accomplish this. Teachers could comment weekly on these journals, highlighting why students might have been successful—reinforcing positive habits that can continue to grow their intelligence. These journals can be kept in an online forum so that students have access to them at home and at school—without fear of losing them in the hallway, their lockers, the bus, and so on.

COVERT INSTRUCTIONAL DECISIONS AT SCHOOL FOR BUILDING COMMUNITY AND A GROWTH MINDSET

Flexible Grouping

Flexible Grouping is the use of multiple grouping strategies in a relatively short amount of time. Although certainly applicable to at-home "groupings" as well, the primary use and impact of Flexible Grouping, will be realized at school. In a flexibly grouped classroom, students are not taken aback by working in a small group of students because they do so with great frequency and in a variety of configurations. For example, over the course of several days, teachers might purposefully group students based on readiness patterns (both same and mixed readiness) or interests. These groupings require planning and alignment with instructional goals, and we examine each of these grouping configurations in more detail in forthcoming chapters.

> In a flexibly grouped classroom, students are not taken aback by working in a small group of students because they do so with great frequency and in a variety of configurations.

FIGURE 2.1: "ME" POSTCARDS

1. **Jar of Pickles**—The go-to gift for anyone to give me during the holidays. I love pickles, and Vlasic really does have the best crunch.

2. **Ballroom Dancers**—Dancing is one of my favorite hobbies—and the only time I look graceful!

3. **NoBo/Hiker (North Bound Hiker)**—It is my dream to hike the Appalachian Trail after I graduate.

4. **World Map**—I love the idea of traveling to different cultures and parts of the world, and of course as an Earth Science major I have a huge appreciation for the planet.

5. **Cat**—My 12-year-old best friend named Cookie. Every time I go home I have photo shoots with her and I am well past the point of "crazy cat lady" with her.

SOURCE: Used with permission of Kira Heeschen.

1. **Connecticut**—This is my home state so I drew my 5 family members (Mom, Dad, Kyle, Logan, Jordan) as stick figures representing how much my family and where I come from means to me.

2. $\sqrt{(-1)}$ ♥ **Math**—The square root of -1 is i so the statement reads: "I love math." I wanted to be a math teacher (specifically algebra and geometry) since I was in fourth grade.

3. **Gymnast**—I have done gymnastics since age 2 and competed since age 7. I am currently on the Club Gymnastics team and hold the position as treasurer.

4. **Books**—I like to read in my free time and I love the *Harry Potter* books. I have reread them every summer for the past 5 years.

5. **Mickey**—I am a huge Disney fan. I am currently collecting all of the Disney movies on DVD.

SOURCE: Used with permission of Brittany French.

FIGURE 2.2: EIGHTH-GRADE ELA CLASS TWO-SIDED JOURNAL

Standard:
CCSS.ELA-LITERACY.W.8.1.B
Support claim(s) with logical reasoning and relevant evidence, using accurate, credible sources and demonstrating an understanding of the topic or text.

What I Achieved Today That Took Effort, and Why I Was Able to Achieve It	Teacher Comments and Feedback
When we first started this unit I never thought I would be able to distinguish between credible sources and less credible ones. However, I tried out a comparing and contrasting strategy using a graphic organizer and got much better at it!	That's a great strategy to use when trying to analyze something! I bet you could also use that in our next unit when we investigate persuasion, because a big part of that is analyzing what makes an effective persuasive piece.

It is also reasonable for teachers to more frequently group students based on lower-stakes methods such as student choice, "randomized" grouping strategies (discussed in Chapter 6), or through informal methods involving student commonalities. Consider the following examples:

1. "Fold the Line" (Doubet & Hockett, 2015): Students line up across the front of the room according to a nonacademic factor. Examples include

- *Numerically* by the last four digits of their phone numbers.
- *Chronologically* according to birthday.
- *Light spectrum order* (ROY G BIV) according to their favorite color or by the color they are wearing.
- *Preference order* according to how much they like Italian food, reality television, and so on.

Once students are in line, the teacher can form pairs or groups by "clumping" students according to how they are placed in the line (i.e., two to four students standing next to one another) OR the teacher can "fold the line" so that students are working with others who are at the opposite end of the spectrum. These groups are easily formed and should be used for tasks that require no particular expertise. For example, a science teacher could use ROY G BIV order to quickly form teams for an in-class investigation or test review.

2. "Four Corners" (Kagan & Kagan, 2009): The teacher numbers each of the classroom corners and assigns a different factor to each before asking students to move to the corner that best represents their preference. For example, an English teacher could assign the four corners as follows:

- Move to Corner 1 if you prefer action movies (e.g., *Transformers, Big Hero 6*).

- Move to Corner 2 if you prefer animated features (e.g., *Frozen, Toy Story*).

- Move to Corner 3 if you prefer comedies (e.g., *The Lego Movie, Paul Blart: Mall Cop*).

- Move to Corner 4 if you prefer sci-fi films (e.g., *X-Men, Ender's Game*).

Once in their corners, students divide into smaller groups of three to four students each (if necessary) and move to a suitable work area in the room where they work together to compile a list of the character traits/qualities/behaviors that constitute a "Hero" in their chosen kind of movie.

3. "Team Huddles": A teacher can call a "Team Huddle" anytime he or she desires to work with a small group of students. This policy should be explained upfront and then instituted in a variety of ways so that it is not seen as a stigma. A history teacher might call a Team Huddle for the following reasons:

- To discuss a current event that corresponds to an area of interest of a small group of students as revealed in a community-building activity or conversation.

- To answer a question raised by only a few students on an exit card.

- To give makeup work to students who were absent.

- To ask clarifying questions about a blog post.

- To clarify a misconception revealed in an assignment.

- To provide an alternative discussion question to students who demonstrated unusual insight during a class discussion.

Varying the grouping of students in this manner builds community because students get to know one another and discover their common interests in the process. Furthermore, it gets learners used to working with virtually every member of their class. It builds community by bonding students through shared experiences, and it fosters the growth mindset because students do not see themselves pigeonholed into one "kind" of student working in any one "kind" of group. They can always learn something from their classmates . . . and their classmates can always learn something

> If Team Huddles are used frequently and with alternating purposes, no student should be consistently *included* in or *excluded* from them. The huddle should be seen as just another informal means of communicating with students.

from them! A tenth-grade student reflecting on his experience in a flexibly grouped classroom remarked, "You can get help from other people around you and so you don't feel like you're either superior or inferior to anyone else . . . it all kind of mixes and we all work together" (Doubet, 2007, p. 239). This mindset is a crucial component of the successfully flipped, differentiated classroom; however, it does not develop without purposeful cultivation using both Flexible Grouping and other proactive measures as pruning tools.

OVERT AT-HOME ACTIVITIES FOR BUILDING COMMUNITY AND A GROWTH MINDSET

In a flipped classroom, teachers use videos or other instructional techniques to deliver content at home. Teachers can also use this method to help build classroom community and mindset at the beginning of the year and periodically throughout their time with the students.

There are many great videos that can help build community and foster a growth mindset in students. Below we identify several examples followed by ideas for how teachers might structure at-home processing assignments to build community and develop a growth mindset in students. An overarching principle of this book is that we must ask students to do more than passively watch instructional videos. We believe this principle holds true for community-building videos as well. In succeeding chapters, we present many activities to help students process and reflect on what they are learning from online, at-home instruction. In this chapter, we present ideas and questions that might be used to help students actively process ideas about collaboration, community, and the growth mindset.

Community Videos

1. *The Myth of Average TEDx Talk (http://tedxtalks.ted.com/video/The-Myth-of-Average-Todd-Rose-a):* In this video, L. Todd Rose, a high school dropout and Harvard Professor, uses the example of cockpit design for fighter pilots to make the case that there is no "average," rather that successful cockpits should be "designed to the edges." In these designs, adjustable seats and other movable parts helped to make the cockpits more accessible for a larger number of pilots, increasing the talent pool for our military (including women). He then connects this to the classroom, arguing that all students have a "jagged learning profile," with varying strengths and needs, and that the most effective environments embrace and plan for these differences.

2. *Google Forms for Teacher and Student Interaction (https://www.youtube.com/watch?v=2Y0Gm02XGis):* This clip profiles a high school teacher who uses Google Forms to interact with her students and provide them with an way to share feelings about

their lives, school, or other topics of importance to them. For students who struggle to trust adults, this method serves as a gateway to fostering stronger teacher-student relationships both inside and outside the school building.

3. Embracing Differences on TeacherTube.com (http://www.teachertube.com/video/embracing-differences-221412): This video documents a school struggling to come to grips with the death of a student who was the victim of a hate crime. Teachers use artwork as a learning tool to help students reflect on the value of community and diversity in their lives. The efforts of teachers, administrators, and community officials are highlighted to provide context for these efforts.

Community Questions

After watching any of the videos described above, students can discuss the following questions in blogs, discussion boards, in a Google Form, and so on.

- What does it mean to be part of a community? Why do people align themselves with communities?

- What is one community you are part of that makes you feel valued? Why? How can we capture that same feeling of value in our class?

- What have you learned about the various strengths and needs of your classmates? How might this change your perception of and interaction with one another?

Mindset Videos

1. Famous Failures (https://www.youtube.com/watch?v=zLYECIjmnQs): This brief video profiles famous people who have experienced great success in their lives in various areas (sports, entertainment, science, etc.). The unique twist is that the video introduces each person first by listing his or her (usually unknown) failures. The message behind this video is that to be successful it is important to view failure as part of the process of eventual success—that we often learn more from failure than we do being successful all the time.

2. Grit TED Talk (http://www.ted.com/talks/angela_lee_duckworth_the_key_to_success_grit?language=en): Teacher-turned-psychologist Angela Lee Duckworth discusses her work researching success and her discovery that the biggest predictor of success is "grit," not innate talent. She describes grit as a combination of several attributes, including passion, perseverance, stamina, and hard work (Duckworth, 2013). She goes on to describe her research in Chicago Public Schools where she administered a questionnaire to students to gauge their grit and found that "grittier" students were significantly more likely to graduate. The important take-away is that failure isn't permanent; it is only a temporary condition. A video like this can help students better understand the role of perseverance in learning and success.

3. Gospel For Teens (60 Minutes Segment from April, 2011) (This video is available in two parts: http://www.cbsnews.com/videos/gospel-for-teens-part-1/ and http://www.cbsnews.com/videos/gospel-for-teens-part-2/): CBS's *60 Minutes* profiles a choir based in Harlem called "Gospel for Teens." The segment follows the choir, along with their director, Vy Higginsen, from students' initial selection to the "beginners" choir in the fall, to their large concert in the spring. In addition to the joy of watching an entire group of inner city young people come together and beat the odds stacked against them, the viewer is also privy to the personal growth of several students—one who struggles to simply say her name on stage, and another who uses the choir as a means of filling a void of parental support. But what is most apparent watching this segment is the power that the growth mindset has on success, both for the members of the choir and their director. It is this attitude in the face of resistance that helps these students—and their teacher—persevere.

4. The Near Miss TED Talk (https://www.ted.com/talks/sarah_lewis_embrace_the_near_win?language=en): In this video, historian and writer Sarah Lewis discusses the value of the near misses in our lives. Said differently, how do we view our "almost-failures"? Do we see them as opportunities to work toward mastery and push forward, or as roadblocks that prevent us from progressing? She argues that our success is largely dependent on how we handle these situations in our lives.

Mindset Questions

After watching any of the videos described above, students can discuss the following questions in blogs, discussion boards, in a Google Form, and so on.

- Describe a time when you failed at something initially, but then with effort became more successful. If you can't think of a time, picture something that you are struggling with now. What steps might you need to take to become more successful?

- Do you believe that intelligence is a product of nature or nurture? Why?

- Select one of the "famous failures" that most resonates with you. Why? What can you learn from this on a personal level? Try to be as specific as possible.

COVERT AT-HOME STUDENT INTERACTIONS FOR BUILDING COMMUNITY IN ACADEMIC CONTEXTS

The videos and questions described above provide teachers with the means to structure virtual peer-to-peer interactions with the goal of fostering a supportive classroom community. As mentioned in Chapter 1, learning is supported when students are able to process information *socially*. The tone of this social interaction can be shaped by deliberately discussing mindset and community both at home and at school. But students also need support in transitioning from interaction about *social matters* (e.g., community and mindset) to interactions about *academic matters*. The nature of at-home interaction becomes fundamentally different when students redirect their attention to discussing their grasp of content. Remaining chapters provide specific strategies for teachers to use to encourage positive academic interactions among students at home. But it is helpful to think proactively about how to structure and monitor both *how* and *with whom* students will interact in an online fashion.

Giving Feedback

It is imperative for the teacher of a flipped classroom to set and post guidelines for what is acceptable with virtual comments, just as he or she would for comments made in class. For example, teachers might let students know that they must give "Two Glows and a Grow," where each student must identify two aspects he or she liked about the blog post and something that the writer might consider working on or improving for future posts. When writing glows and grows, however, the students should maintain a respectful tone and employ effective feedback techniques that avoid opinions or other subjective comments. "I feel like" should not be an acceptable way to start their response.

Among his recommendations for effective feedback, Wiggins (2012) notes that comments should be

1. **Goal Referenced:** Remind students about the goal when giving feedback.

2. **Actionable:** Provide useful, concrete information to show students specific steps they could take to improve.

3. **Timely:** The sooner the feedback, the better so that students can make adjustments while in the process of learning a concept.

So what does this kind of feedback look like in action? Examples of effective feedback that adhere to these guidelines follow, based on math students' blogging about solving problems using the order of operations. Specifically, students were asked to solve two problems using the order of operations and then explain the process they used to solve it. Last, they were instructed to write about a daily event in their lives where following a precise order is essential to completing the event or action successfully.

> It is imperative for the teacher of a flipped classroom to set and post guidelines for what is acceptable with virtual comments, just as he or she would for comments made in class.

1. **Goal Referenced:** Student feedback to peer: "The goal was to apply the order of operations to correctly solve problems, but you added before you multiplied."

2. **Actionable:** Student feedback to peer: "Parentheses come before exponents, which is something that you missed here. Make sure you remember that in future problems, or you'll mess up the rest of your good math!"

3. **Timely:** Teacher direction to students: "Make sure you provide feedback to each other on the same afternoon or evening that you are posting your own blog response."

Clearly, such directed feedback takes practice. To help ensure that students master the art of providing each other with respectful, helpful feedback, teachers should devote ample time to providing this kind of feedback themselves, having students practice giving such feedback to each other, and exploring examples and nonexamples of effective feedback. In addition, some class time can be devoted to students who have questions about feedback. It is likely that—despite our best efforts—some negative or even incorrect feedback will be given. These situations actually present excellent teaching moments for students who might be confused about the content or about how to respond to errors. By being thoughtful and purposeful with how students interact virtually, teachers can lay a solid foundation for positive exchanges among all students, building a healthy virtual classroom community in the process.

Ensuring That ALL Students Connect

So how can a teacher ensure that students respond to all their classmates rather than only to those they consider to be their friends? Teachers might use a table like that in Figure 2.3 to assign and monitor student-to-student interactions via comments on classmates' blog posts. Students respond to each other's posts when their *assignment numbers* line up (in this case, assignment numbers align with blog posts 1–6). So in Week 1 Amelie and Josh would comment on each other's posts, in Week 2 Amelie and Sarah would respond to each other's posts, and so on. It's important to note that this class has an even number of students, so interactions disperse evenly. With an odd number of students, the teacher might need to group students in threes and have them comment on each other's posts.

FIGURE 2.3: RECORD OF STUDENT-STUDENT BLOG-POST INTERACTIONS

	Josh	Amelie	Carlos	Monique	Axel	Sarah
Josh	X	1	2	3	4	5
Amelie	1	X	3	4	5	2
Carlos	2	3	X	5	1	4
Monique	3	4	5	X	2	1
Axel	4	5	1	2	X	3
Sarah	5	2	4	1	3	X

Using a structured system like this prevents the formation of online cliques because it requires all students in a class to respond to each one of their classmates at least once.

THE BOTTOM LINE

Teachers should make every effort to develop community and mindset both at home and at school. For a learning environment to be most effective—regardless of where this environment is located—students must feel valued. They must come to view errors as part of the learning process and seek challenge with the understanding that the classroom community is in place to provide a safety net of support. This chapter has presented numerous ways for teachers looking to create a differentiated flipped classroom to promote an effective place for learning, both face-to-face and virtually. In the next chapter, we discuss methods in which teachers can increase their knowledge of their students' learning needs through the use of ongoing assessment.

> For a learning environment to be most effective—regardless of where this environment is located—students must feel valued. They must come to view errors as part of the learning process and seek challenge with the understanding that the classroom community is in place to provide a safety net of support.

A TEACHER IN ACTION

Ms. Velazquez knew that she would need to start getting students comfortable with one another both online and in class if she was going to make the most of the flexibility afforded by her flipped classroom. She began by asking students Attendance Questions—such as "McDonald's or Burger King?"—on their arrival to class and tallying results to use as data for in-class math problems. She branched out to asking attendance-type questions on discussion boards and assigning students to comment on their classmates' posts. When she noticed that students were commenting only on their friends' posts, she made the rule that each student must comment on the posts of three classmates who had last names that began with letters contained in their *own* first names. These measures alone seemed to increase student-student interactions in and outside class.

To both capitalize on and increase student interactions in class, Ms. Velazquez began Folding the Line to create in-class groupings for "video reviews" and practice around concepts introduced in the previous night's online tutorials. She lined students up by the square of their birth month on one day, by the sum of the last four digits of their phone numbers the next, and so on. Sometimes she made groups of four according to who was standing next to whom in the line; other times she made pairs by folding the line. It wasn't long before students came to expect the unexpected.

Once students were used to working in groups, Ms. Velazquez was able to be more deliberate about her groupings. She called several Team Huddles per class period to discuss questions and misconceptions students made in their homework and class work. She began noticing that many students repeatedly made the same mistakes in their work and decided this phenomenon needed attention regarding both academics and mindset. Accordingly, she assigned students the "Famous Failures" video to watch at home and required that they respond with discussion posts about the most "famous failures"—or common mistakes—they had been making during their current unit (on Order of Operations). She grouped students with like answers together to make videos (in class) depicting how to avoid these "famous math failures." The class watched all the videos together to serve as a review before the unit test. She was encouraged to see her students had bonded in school and at home in both nonacademic AND academic ways.

NOTE: Bolded terms indicate strategies discussed earlier in the chapter.

CHAPTER 3

Using Formative Assessment to Check for Understanding

For students to succeed in a flipped instructional environment, teachers must *respond* to learner needs. But simply being "responsive" isn't enough to facilitate growth for every student; rather, success hinges on "the recognition, articulation, and commitment to plan for student differences" (Tomlinson, 2005). In other words, teachers must be *proactive* in discovering students' learning needs and in planning to address those needs. This is where the typical approach to the flipped classroom model may fall short regarding differentiation and teachers' ability to manage meeting a variety of needs in an nontraditional setting; flipped classrooms often operate on a strictly reactive basis, which can lead many teachers to feel thinly spread.

A TEACHER IN ACTION: PART 1

Ms. Velazquez, whom we met in the first two chapters, was feeling overextended when she first began experimenting with the Flipped model. As she worked to foster a healthy sense of community among her students—both at home and at school—she began to get a general feel for what her students needed to be productive and to feel successful. She could respond to some learner needs by using small group reviews; this was certainly progress! But there were still points in her units when Ms. Velazquez knew her students were in vastly different places and that her minor adjustments were not sufficient to bridge these wide gaps. Furthermore, she felt overwhelmed with how to gauge exactly who needed what. It was becoming increasingly clear to her that she needed to employ more proactive methods of *formative assessment*.

FORMATIVE VERSUS SUMMATIVE

The word *assessment* is typically associated with tests or projects, which are traditionally administered at the end of the instructional cycle to present a final picture of what students have mastered. This conception reflects only one kind of assessment: summative. *Summative assessment* tells us how students performed in a "rearview mirror" manner; we see their results as we proceed to the next unit. *Formative assessment*, on the other hand, gives us "front windshield" information; it serves as "a GPS for student learning" (Stiggins & Chappuis, 2012, p. 12). In other words, it lets teachers know what is needed to help students succeed while there is still time to impact their learning. Formative assessment is the key to success in a differentiated classroom, and it's the secret to efficiency in a flipped classroom; in both cases, it lets the teacher make "up-front" plans about how to address learning diversity in a timely fashion.

> Formative assessment is the key to success in a differentiated classroom, and it's the secret to efficiency in a flipped classroom; in both cases, it lets the teacher make "up-front" plans about how to address learning diversity in a timely fashion.

In this chapter, we have outlined a variety of strategies for monitoring student understanding. Although we have grouped them as methods to use at home and at school, in truth, many of the strategies can be used effectively in either setting. Bottom line: whether at home or in school, a teacher must proactively identify student learning needs to make efficient use of the flipped classroom's opportunities to differentiate based on readiness.

QUICK WAYS TO ASSESS FOR READINESS AT HOME

The flipped classroom model often requires students to watch recorded lectures or demonstrations at home as preparation for in-school processing assignments. In truth, processing should actually begin *at home while engaging with the lecture*. The most natural and obvious way to facilitate this is to ask student to pause the lecture, rewind and re-watch necessary portions, and so on. This is a necessary first step, but if we stop there, we have not asked students to fully engage their minds in the learning process. "Next step processing" activities require students to cognitively invest as they watch the lecture, demonstration, and so on. An example of such an exercise is the "Problems and Possibilities" format (see Figure 3.1). This four-category organizer can guide students to actively participate in the lecture while monitoring their thinking in the process. Not only is such metacognition vital to the learning process (Bransford, Brown, & Cocking, 2000; Hattie, 2012), but it also prepares students to accurately assess their own readiness to tackle material while providing teachers with concrete evidence that can either support or refute students' self-assessments. Students can post their responses online or bring them to class the following day; either way, their responses provide data that can be used to drive next steps in the learning process, whether that's a chance to work more with the content or to tunnel more deeply into the possibilities they've articulated.

FIGURE 3.1: PROBLEMS AND POSSIBILITIES CHART

My **Solutions** (with work shown)	My **Answers** (to lecture questions)
Some **Possibilities** (What makes sense about this content? How might I use it?)	Potential **Problems** (Things that stumped me; Things I'm not confident about.)

Graphic Organizers

The "Problems and Possibilities" chart pictured above is one example of using a graphic—or a "nonlinguistic representation"—to guide student learning. Research shows that students' use of nonlinguistic representations to organize and process information has positive effects on their learning (Dean, Hubbell, Pitler, & Stone, 2012). In particular, strategies that help students note patterns in sequence, process (cause and effect), or concept/principle relationships can enable students to more effectively retain and utilize new knowledge (Dean et al., 2012). Jim Burke's *Tools for Thought* (2002) offers a rich supply of such organizers for use in classrooms of various grade levels and content areas. Additionally, there is a wealth of online resources for teachers who are looking for graphic organizers to facilitate student learning. One such resource is the website edhelper.com, which includes resources such as the following:

"Cause and Effect" (http://www.edhelperclipart.com/clipart/teachers/org-1cause1 effect.pdf): Used with a science demonstration, students can record their reflections on a lab experiment. For more fact-based lectures (e.g., social studies), students can record key people, places, times, and events on one side of the organizer and the significance of each on the opposite side. In either case, students should conclude their processing by recording one overarching take-away and one lingering question on the back.

"Cycle" (http://www.edhelperclipart.com/clipart/teachers/org-cycle6.pdf): Ideal for science lectures and problem-solving procedures, students record the cycle's components inside the circle and record information about how those components affect each other on the periphery. Questions and insights can be included on the back.

> Online forums provide the greatest potential for feedback, as students can get real-time responses from their classmates AND the teacher can come to class armed with issues he or she needs to address.

For each of these organizers, students are engaged in the cognitive work of representing patterns in nonlinguistic formats; this increases learning AND provides rich opportunities for feedback. Students can post their work online in a chat or discussion board forum or bring their work to class with them the following day. Online forums provide the greatest potential for feedback, because students can get real-time responses from their classmates AND the teacher can come to class armed with issues he or she needs to address (overarching questions, trouble spots, or differentiated follow-up tasks for students at different places in their processing). The next best scenario is for teachers to build in time at the beginning of class for students to share their processing sheets, with the understanding that teachers will monitor those discussions and develop groupings/tasks based on student feedback. Clearly, graphic organizers have the potential to serve as both a learning tool for students and as a source of assessment data for teachers in a flipped classroom.

QUICK WAYS TO ASSESS FOR STUDENT READINESS AT SCHOOL

One of the primary benefits of using the Flipped model is increased class time to answer questions and guide student processing. The challenge, however, is how to use this class time *efficiently* to truly address the myriad of challenges students encounter. The graphic organizers discussed earlier guide students' work while they are at home. In addition, there are strategies teachers can employ to gauge student learning after they've arrived at school. Asking, "What questions do you have?" is a good—and important—first step, but it should not be the last—or only—step. Too often, students either don't know how to articulate their questions or are unaware they even have questions/misconceptions; in other words, "students do not always know what they think they know" (Willingham, 2003/2004, p. 48). There are several quick and easy strategies that teachers can use with individual students and groups of students in a flipped classroom to monitor student understanding and determine how to adjust instruction accordingly.

Individual Formative Assessments

Entrance Prompts and Activities: When students enter class after completing an at-home learning experience (e.g., lab or lecture video), teachers can begin the period by asking students to complete an Entrance Prompt. This entrance prompt should contain a few questions designed to probe thinking and elicit responses that would help both the teacher and the students know how to proceed in the learning process. Entrance questions should provide students with the chance to share something they've learned, but also to "prove" that they learned it by applying it (procedurally, contextually, personally, etc.).

Consider the prompt in Figure 3.2 (aligned to CCSS.ELA-LITERACY.RST.11–12.7: *Integrate and evaluate multiple sources of information presented in diverse formats and media*):

This entrance activity does more than simply reveal whether students know the meaning of the terms *reliable* and *unreliable*; rather, it asks them to *apply their knowledge* to evaluate potential resources. Such information—when discussed as a class— can help both teacher and students determine who is ready to begin research and who needs more time sifting through sources and discussing their merits.

FIGURE 3.2: SOURCE RELIABILITY "ENTRANCE ACTIVITY"

Source	Reliable or Unreliable?	Why?
Forums		
Blogs		
Peer-Reviewed Articles		
Scholarly Articles		
Facebook		
Scientific Journals		

SOURCE: Used with permission of Joseph Wieland.

The algebra Entrance questions featured in Figure 3.3 (aligned to CCSS.MATH .CONTENT.HSA.REI.A.1: *Understand solving equations as a process of reasoning and explain the reasoning*) provide similar opportunities for students to demonstrate their thinking. The first question allows the teacher to probe deeper into students' thinking to see if they can reason and explain problem solving mathematically rather than simply solving the problem. Student responses allowed the teacher to discern who simply needed more help with the operational aspects of the content (e.g., several failed to discuss the negative; others did not discuss collecting like terms) and who failed to grasp the content conceptually (e.g., several students made calculation errors *and* simply listed "FOIL" rather than truly explaining their thinking). The teacher was able to see who needed more practice and who was ready to apply this knowledge to more complex, life-application problems.

FIGURE 3.3: MATH ENTRANCE PROMPTS

Describe to me (using words, not numbers!) how to simplify the expression. Be specific and use math words!

$$(x + 3)(x - 5)$$

About what part of your explanation are you least confident? Why?

SOURCE: Used with permission of Gabrielle Gardner.

3–2–1 Prompts: Many teachers embrace the 3–2–1 format for Entrance (and Exit) prompts because it provides a framework with which students can become familiar and comfortable. As is the case with all formative assessments, however, the questions must be phrased in such a way as to elicit useful responses. In the example below (Figure 3.4, aligned to CCSS ELA-LITERACY.W.5.3.B: *Use narrative techniques, such as dialogue, description, and pacing, to develop experiences and events or show the responses of characters to situations*), all three questions are designed to reveal specific aspects of student learning. The first question reveals what information students retained from their at-home learning experience; the second question taps into their ability to use this knowledge; the last question probes—in an inviting manner—lingering questions or points of confusion.

FIGURE 3.4: 3–2–1 ELA ENTRANCE PROMPTS

Name **3** narrative techniques a writer can use to show what a character is like.

Use **2** of these techniques to briefly describe yourself.

List **1** technique you hope the teacher will discuss in more detail today.

Padlet.com: This website allows teachers to make entrance tickets virtual, visual, sortable, and mobile. Teachers can craft an entrance question to post on a virtual "board" and then share it with students via a web address or a QR code. Students log on to the Padlet board, click on the screen, and type in their response. They can also drag files from their desktop onto the board. As students post responses, they will become visible on the screen. These responses—appearing in text boxes—can then be dragged and sorted—via mouse, touchscreen, or Smartboard—allowing both the teacher and the students to examine responses and determine patterns. Padlet.com can also serve as an excellent tool for formative assessment at home.

"My Favorite No": This formative entrance activity is a technique demonstrated on the Teaching Channel (https://www.teachingchannel.org/videos/class-warm-up-routine) by Leah Alcala, a math teacher at Martin Luther King Middle School in Berkeley, CA. She uses a technique entitled "My Favorite No." This reflective strategy is aligned to CCSS.MATH.CONTENT.HSA.REI.A.1 (*Understand solving equations as a process of reasoning and explain the reasoning*) and features the following steps:

1. Teacher poses an opening question OR consults student responses posted to Padlet, a discussion forum, or other digital tool the night before (see additional information on this tool in Appendix A).

2. Teacher chooses a common and critical error in student work to highlight.

3. Teacher displays the response/error at the beginning of class and explains to students that it's her "Favorite No" because (1) it highlights a key learning point that many students confuse, and (2) it features some "good math" along with the mistake.

4. The teacher leads the class in discussion of what's been done correctly in the problem, and then moves to an error analysis.

5. All students complete a similar problem to show that they can avoid the mistake, or "Favorite No," in their future work.

This strategy not only supplies the teacher with a rich source of information about students' grasp of the material, but it also provides students with a means of reflecting on their mistakes and using that knowledge to move forward in the learning process. At the same time, it sends the important message that mistakes are a necessary part of learning (Bransford et al., 2000) and that they should be celebrated and examined rather than hidden and dismissed.

Frayer Diagram: A Frayer Diagram (Frayer, Frederick, & Klausmeier, 1969) can provide a useful structure for Entrance Prompts. The classic Frayer Diagram features a four-square organizer that asks students to provide the **definition** of a concept, its **importance**, some crystallizing **examples**, and some **nonexamples** that may be frequently confused with examples. Figure 3.5 (a preassessment designed to gauge student readiness for CCSS.ELA-LITERACY.RH.6–8.1: *Cite specific textual evidence to support analysis of primary and secondary sources*) illustrates the use of the classic Frayer Diagram.

FIGURE 3.5: CLASSIC FRAYER DIAGRAM

Primary Source	
Definition	Importance/Use
Examples (and why)	Related Nonexamples (and why)

The categories of the classic Frayer Diagram make sense used in conjunction with the ELA/history standard above; it is important for students to be able to understand the value of primary sources when analyzing historical events, and also to distinguish what qualifies as a primary source of information. For some learning goals, however, these categories are not the most efficient. In such instances, the categories of the diagram can be altered to better assess the leaning targets. Figure 3.6 illustrates how the strategy can be adjusted to assess student grasp of NGSS MS–LS3 Heredity: Inheritance and Variation of Traits.

In this diagram, the bottom categories allow students to demonstrate that they can make sense of the Punnett square they constructed in the top, which provides the teacher with insight into student thinking and processing.

FIGURE 3.6: ADJUSTED SCIENCE FRAYER DIAGRAM

Genetics	
Make a Punnett Square for two hybrid parents.	
What ratio of the offspring will share their parents' phenotype? Explain.	What ratio of the offspring will share their parents' genotype? Explain.

Elevator Speech: In the world of advertising, there is often a limited amount of time to make a strong sales pitch—perhaps the length of an elevator ride. The Elevator Speech format models this reality for students by asking them to synthesize the most important information from a lesson and present it in a brief amount of time (about 30 seconds). After students write down key points from the lesson in the form of a speech, the teacher asks them to turn to their elbow partner and "sell" the lesson. Once done, the partner then delivers his or her own brief speech. Students then have 30 additional seconds to add any new ideas to their speeches before turning them in or posting them online via any of the forums discussed in Appendix A (e.g., Periscope). This allows the teacher to determine what ideas were gleaned from the lesson and also provides students with opportunities to practice their speaking skills.

Entrance activities like those described above can bridge the gap that sometimes emerges in a flipped classroom between what students viewed or completed at home and what they are ready to wrestle with in class. The teacher can use the results of entrance activities to address learning gaps and strides that result from the different manners and speeds of processing demonstrated by students as they crunched on material at home.

Exit Activities: It may be, however, that further gaps emerge as students wrestle with material **in** class. Because of this very real possibility, teachers may need to gather evidence to help plan differentiated at-home learning experiences (described in Chapter 4). If this is the case, any of the entrance assessment methods discussed above can be used during lesson closure to determine what level of task is appropriate for each student.

Group Formative Assessments

It is also necessary to check in with students throughout the course of instruction to ensure they are progressing appropriately in their learning. Students may begin small group work immediately, putting to use the learning acquired at home the previous evening. After a chunk of work time, the class can stop and complete processing activities that serve to showcase what the class—as a whole—has grasped, as well as with what it is struggling.

Cries for Help: A routine that requires very little prep—but that can reap generous rewards—is the establishment of "Help Stations," "Help Cards/Cups," or "Self-Help Groups." The goal of each of these activities is to use in-class work time—whether completed individually or in groups—in a more efficient manner.

Help Stations: Serve as "holding areas" for students with questions. Students who find themselves stuck can move to designated areas of the room and wait for the teacher to come address their questions. When the teacher arrives, he or she finds that (a) the same question can be addressed once rather than multiple times as he or she circulates through the room, and/or that (b) students have talked among themselves and answered their own questions. Either way, it allows for a more efficient use of instructional time.

Help Cards/Cups: Students display colored cards or cups as needed during individual or group work. The teacher can survey the room and call all students with a help signal displayed to a corner of the room; alternatively, if many help cards/cups are displayed, the teacher can pause and address questions full group. (*Note:* See this strategy in action at https://www.teachingchannel.org/videos/show-your-cards-student-assessment)

Self-Help Groups: Students self-select to hear info another way or to work with a new application. The teacher creates stations featuring appropriate websites or other resources for particular topics, and students move to use resources as needed during in-class processing time.

Quartet Quiz: This technique, developed by Tomlinson (2005), features individual thought, work in teams of four, full-class discussion, and individual reflection. In the process, the teacher is able to survey the class to see what students have learned and with what they are still struggling. Most importantly, teachers can address questions as they arise and squelch misconceptions on the spot. The steps of a Quartet Quiz (see Figure 3.7) include the following:

1. Teacher poses a question.

2. Students write/prepare responses.

3. Students meet in quads and check answers.

4. "Summarizer" reports: "We know" and "We wonder" statements.

5. Teacher takes notes/records student answers on board (*Note:* Steps 4 and 5 can be condensed into one step by utilizing Padlet or Socrative posts. Each summarizer submits his or her group's "We know" and "We wonder" statements digitally).

6. Class discusses "We wonder" statements and teacher ensures all questions are answered.

7. Class develops closure/clarification/summary statements.

After using the Quartet Quiz featured in Figure 3.7, the teacher of this classroom would know exactly what to clarify and review (e.g., examples of a relation that is a function and a relation that is not a function) and what to address next (e.g., graphing the ordered pairs from the function and the nonfunction and examining the differing results; offering a situation that makes the math less theoretical and more practical). The Quartet Quiz took the guesswork out of how well students understood the video and directed the teacher's "next steps" in instruction.

FIGURE 3.7: SAMPLE MATH QUARTET QUIZ RESULTS

Quartet Quiz used after students watched a Khan Academy video on relations and functions:

We THINK We Know . . .	We Wonder . . .
The Domain of a function is the set of all values that x can be substituted for (input).	Inputs and outputs? What does this have to do with xs and ys? Why these terms?
The Range of a function is the set of values (y) that the function can produce (output).	How can he say a function has a "one-to-one" relationship if a number in the range (x) has more than one number in the domain (y) mapped to it?
Relation—set of ordered pairs	
Function—a relation that has a one-to-one relationship between the domain and the range. Given a member of the domain (x), you should be able to tell exactly what number in the range (y) it maps to.	What do functions and relations have to do with graphing? He talked about x- and y-intercepts in the video, but we never saw the connection . . .
All functions are relations but not all relations are functions.	This may be related to the other group's question (above), but what does this actually mean? WHY aren't all relations also functions (other than the fact that they don't have a one-to-one correspondence)?

Graffiti/Carousel: This popular cooperative learning strategy (Kagan & Kagan, 2009) can be "retooled" to check for understanding and monitor student misconceptions. The process involved the following steps:

1. Post poster paper at different spots in room, each paper featuring a different question or prompt.

2. Each group receives a different colored marker and begins at one of the posters.

3. Students move in small groups and work to compile information in response to prompts/problems posted on each sheet of poster paper.

4. Students write all they know about the question, spending a limited amount of time at each station to record thoughts.

5. Time is called and groups rotate. At new station, the new group first "codes" information generated by other groups:

   ✓ = Agreed. We considered that, too!

   ! = New idea—we didn't think about that.

   ? = We don't understand OR we don't agree with that (must explain *why*).

6. The new group then adds new material to the information already recorded by other groups.

7. With every rotation, the recorder in the group changes.

8. Rotation continues until every group has rotated through every poster.

9. The teacher circulates through posters, highlighting important responses, answering questions, and addressing misconceptions.

Graffiti/Carousel is a great way to begin and end activities, or to transition between activities. If the activity serves to reinforce previously introduced material, students should refer to their notes, texts, and so on throughout the activity. For example, Graffiti could be used in a science class to determine what students retained from an online tutorial on biomes. The teacher stations five different pieces of poster paper around the room, each labeled with one of the major types of biomes—aquatic, desert, forest, grassland, and tundra. Small groups spread out among the five posters, with each group beginning at a different biome. Students are given a few minutes to list everything they can recall from the tutorial about the *history, distinguishing characteristics, examples,* and different *subtypes* of each biome as well as potential *threats* to each biome (these categories are posted on the board or screen for students to reference). When time is called, groups rotate to the next poster and check the previous group's work. They must code each piece of information to indicate agreement or disagreement, recording questions, if necessary; only then can they add their own ideas to the poster. When time is called, the groups rotate; this rotation continues until all groups have visited each station and ends with students returning to *all* the posters to see how their ideas were challenged, affirmed, and supplemented after they left. The activity requires students to use their notes from the tutorial—along with each other—as necessary resources to complete the task successfully. In addition, it provides the teacher with a means of monitoring at-home viewing, uncovering misconceptions, and discovering where students need more instruction.

Online Status Checks

Teachers also have access to several online methods for gathering group formative assessment data. In addition to Padlet, there are tools such as TodaysMeet, Polleverywhere, and Socrative that facilitate the collection of student responses to questions or polling data. For example, teachers might use Socrative to make a digital exit ticket for small groups to post "one big idea they have and one question that remains" after a group assignment. Or, if teachers are interested in students self-assessing their understanding after a lesson, they might create Polleverywhere survey for students to rate themselves on a scale of 1 to 4, with 4 being "ready to move on," and 1 meaning "I'm stuck in quicksand—throw me a rope!" A more detailed overview of these—and additional—digital formative assessment tools can be found in Appendix A.

THE BOTTOM LINE

The strategies provided in this chapter are designed to help students actively engage in instruction both at home and at school. They also highlight methods by which both teachers and students can monitor understanding in both settings. The next chapter discusses what teachers can do with the information gathered from these formative assessment strategies. It attempts to answer the question, "Once I discover that students are in different places in their learning, what can I do to address these discrepancies in student readiness?"

A TEACHER IN ACTION: PART 2

Ms. Velazquez began mixing in her normal **Fold the Line** activities with "How well did my tutorial click with you?" lineups. One end of the spectrum represented "5—I got all three practice problems right," and the other end represented "0—you lost me during minute 1 of the video." Some days she held Team Huddles with the "5s," giving them next-level challenge problems to complete while she retaught the lesson another way to those who needed it. Other days she huddled with those who had questions and set the others to work on the next assignment. She began asking students to post ah-has and questions via **Padlet** midway through the class period. She often used those responses to maximize the rest of her instructional time.

She also found a way to adapt **Graffiti** to mathematics. She began by posting six different equations around the room for her class working on multistep equations. She then used **Fold the Line** ("Line up according to how much you like veggies on your pizza!") to form groups of four to five students each. Each group began at a different poster/problem and took the first step to solve it, rotating to the next poster/problem when time was called and checking the previous group's work. They had to approve the first step—or correct any errors they noted—before moving on to the next step in solving the equation. When all six equations were solved, students returned to *all* the posters to see if their work was accurate or if/how it had been corrected by their peers. Ms. Velazquez was able to monitor where students needed more instruction to guide them naturally in the process of error analysis.

With these measures in place, Ms. Velazquez began to feel more in touch with where students were in their learning. Granted, the differences that began to emerge often made her wonder what to do next. Group Huddles were a great start, but she knew there must be other ways to more robustly address the diverse learning needs she was discovering through her use of formative assessment.

CHAPTER 4

Differentiating According to Student Readiness

Your students are well aware of the world beyond the classroom, and the role played by their schooling in preparing for the future. Students value being helped to achieve independence and autonomy, and appreciate teachers who can connect the new with the familiar, can convey complex notions in simple terms, who *actively recognize that students learn at different rates, and need varying levels of guidance, feedback, and instruction.*

—Hattie & Yates, 2014, p. 31, emphasis added

Through her use of formative assessment, Ms. Velazquez was discovering not only *that* her students varied in their learning needs, but also *how* those readiness needs differed from day to day. In any lesson, it is common to have students at varying levels of **readiness** tackling the content, and—as Hattie and Yates state above—the successful teacher will be prepared to address those varying readiness needs head-on. The term *readiness* is a fluid term meant to denote where a student is in his or her grasp of learning goals at a certain point in time. It is not synonymous with *ability*, which can imply labels or fixed notions of those who will succeed and those who won't. A student's readiness to learn can vary from lesson to lesson or from skill to skill: students may wrestle with certain concepts but grasp others with ease; students may initially struggle to master a skill, but catch on after much grappling; students may possess an early comprehension of content, but then hit a roadblock and become stumped. As detailed in Chapter 2, teachers with a growth mindset (Dweck, 2006) recognize that with effort and sweat, all students can grow. The term readiness refers to the starting point of that growth, on a particular day, for a particular student. Readiness carries with it the belief that—given the proper feedback and tools for success—every learner can progress. Teachers attending to readiness do not make assumptions about students who "get it" and those who "don't"; rather, they gather evidence—in the form of formative assessment (see Chapter 3 for examples)—to discover exactly what each learner needs to propel him or her to the next step in learning. The ultimate aim of any well-designed activity driven by student readiness is to take learners at least "+1" beyond the students' starting points (Hattie, 2012). Said differently, differentiated activities based on readiness are primarily focused on student growth and based on the realization that—since students start at different points—they will need different instruction to help them grow.

> The term *readiness* is a fluid term meant to denote where a student is in his or her grasp of learning goals at a certain point in time. It is not synonymous with *ability*, which can imply labels or fixed notions of those who will succeed and those who won't.

This chapter explores the following broad categories of instructional strategies to accommodate differences in student readiness:

- Differentiating for Readiness Using Questions and Prompts
- Differentiating for Readiness Through Scaffolding
- Differentiating for Readiness Through Varied Content Delivery

DIFFERENTIATING FOR READINESS USING QUESTIONS AND PROMPTS

Teachers regularly employ a variety of questioning and prompting strategies in the classroom. However, these strategies are often directed heavily toward more able learners (students who are quick to raise their hands), leaving struggling students relegated to the status of bystanders (Lemov, 2010). Further, the majority of questions asked require students to simply recall information rather than to restructure or apply it in some way, even though the latter is a practice that produces additional learning (Hattie & Yates, 2014; Marzano, Pickering, & Pollock, 2001). However, thoughtful planning and implementation of classroom questioning and prompting can raise the levels of participation and achievement among all students (Marzano et al., 2001). To address the various readiness needs of students, teachers of a differentiated flipped classroom should employ effective questioning and prompting strategies both at home and at school that engage different cognitive levels. Below we provide a framework to help teachers conceptualize this process based on Webb's Depth of Knowledge (DOK) Levels (Webb, 2002). Figure 4.1 identifies skills that are associated with each level. In addition, Figures 4.2–4.5 provide sample questions and prompts based on Common Core State Standards (CCSS) and Next Generation Science Standards.

FIGURE 4.1: SKILLS ASSOCIATED WITH EACH KNOWLEDGE LEVEL

One: Recall (Who, What, When, Where, Why)	Identify, List, Recognize, Tell, Recall, Repeat, Define, Calculate, Arrange, State
Two: Skill/Concept	Identify Patterns, Separate, Estimate, If/Then, Observe, Summarize, Categorize, Predict
Three: Strategic Thinking	Revise, Hypothesize, Formulate, Investigate, Construct, Assess, Develop, Appraise
Four: Extended Thinking	Connect, Synthesize, Create, Prove, Apply, Design, Evaluate

NOTE: This is just one framework for conceptualizing degrees of critical thinking. Readers may be more familiar with Bloom's Revised Taxonomy (Anderson et al., 2000). The same structure and guidelines apply regardless of what critical thinking framework is used.

FIGURE 4.2: STANDARDS-ALIGNED EXAMPLE QUESTIONS AND PROMPTS FOR EACH KNOWLEDGE LEVEL—MATH CCSS: GRADE 7

Standard:	
CCSS.MATH.CONTENT.7.EE.B.4 *Use variables to represent quantities in a real-world or mathematical problem and construct simple equations and inequalities to solve problems by reasoning about the quantities.*	
One: Recall **(Who, What, When, Where, Why)**	What does a variable represent?
Two: Skill/Concept	Construct and solve an inequality given certain information.
Three: Strategic Thinking	Based on your understanding of one-variable equations, hypothesize how one might solve equations with two variables.
Four: Extended Thinking	Create a set of five real-world problems where an equation can be used to find an unknown variable. Each real-world problem should apply to what you are currently learning in your other classes (e.g., in PE, determine how many calories you would need daily to maintain your current weight given your age and level of activity).

SOURCE: Used with permission of Stephen Caviness.

Questioning at School

After students have participated in teacher-assigned direct instruction at home, teachers can then plan classroom-questioning strategies that would address diverse readiness needs. It is vital to note that these differentiated questions and prompts must be assigned in response to formative assessment evidence gathered through any of the means discussed in Chapter 3 (e.g., entrance prompts, Padlet responses, Frayer diagrams). We highlight several instructional strategies here that rely on the differentiated prompts and questions illustrated above.

1. Small Group Tasks: The teacher breaks students into small groups based on differing levels of readiness as demonstrated in a formative assessment. Once in these groups, the teacher presents each group with a task card with readiness-appropriate questions. For example, a group of students with highly developed answers on the formative assessment might receive a task card with discussion questions or prompts based on Levels 3 and 4 of Webb's framework. Students with underdeveloped answers—or even misconceptions—on their formative assessments might get a task card with questions and prompts at levels one and two, with at least one level-three question. Including a higher-level question for ALL groups is imperative, since the aim is to take students "+1" above (Hattie, 2012) where they are currently—and since students must "understand facts and ideas in the context of a conceptual framework" to learn (Bransford et al., 2000, p. 16). In other words, teachers should continually find ways to "stretch" student thinking, regardless of their readiness levels. The students discuss their questions in small groups for a set amount of time before the teacher calls the class back together for a discussion about an overarching question that connects all the assigned questions and prompts.

Examples:

- **Science:** Using Figure 4.3, the teacher asks students to respond to the Level 1 question ("What are the parts of an animal cell?") via Kahoot or Socrative and then forms small groups based on students' answers. Students with a strong grasp of the content are paired to discuss the DOK Level 3 question ("Hypothesize what would happen to animals if animal cells had cell walls"), while those students in need of review are paired to discuss the DOK Level 2 question ("Summarize the role of each animal cell part"), with the added instruction to "Make a case for the most important part of an animal cell" (*Note:* This added prompt ensures ALL students are thinking conceptually/considering the cell as a system). Following small group work, the full class

FIGURE 4.3: STANDARDS-ALIGNED EXAMPLE QUESTIONS AND PROMPTS FOR EACH KNOWLEDGE LEVEL—NEXT GENERATION SCIENCE STANDARDS: MIDDLE SCHOOL

Standard:	
MS-LS1–2	
Develop and use a model to describe the function of a cell as a whole and ways in which parts of cells contribute to the function of the cell.	
One: Recall **(Who, What, When, Where, Why)**	What are the parts of an animal cell?
Two: Skill/Concept	Summarize the role of each animal cell part.
Three: Strategic Thinking	Hypothesize what would happen to animals if animal cells had cell walls.
Four: Extended Thinking	Consider the notion of the cell as a system of parts that contribute to its overall function. Create and illustrate an analogy that compares the cell to another system. Be sure to illustrate how the parts of both systems work together effectively.

SOURCE: Used with permission of Stephen Caviness.

considers the DOK Level 4 question: "Create and illustrate an analogy that compares the cell to another system. Be sure to illustrate how the parts of both systems work together effectively."

- **Math:** Using results of an entrance card, the teacher assigns students to one of three tasks to help them take the next step in their learning (based on Wiliam, 2012, p. 34).

  - **Task 1:** You solved all these equations correctly. Now make up three equations for others to solve: one that's harder than those you just solved, one that's at about the same level, and one that's easier. (DOK Level 4)

  - **Task 2:** [This #] of the equations that you solved are incorrect. Find the incorrect solutions and fix them. (DOK Level 3)

  - **Task 3:** You solved these equations incorrectly: _____. Analyze your work to find your errors and fix them. (DOK Level 2/3)

2. Think/Pair/Share: The teacher posts several different questions that address the same learning goal but at different levels of cognitive challenge based on Webb's Depth of Knowledge (*Note:* Posted questions are *not* labeled according to their levels). Students select the question that they feel most ready to discuss. (*Note:* If the teacher notices that some students are consistently opting for the easier questions or prompts when in fact they should be responding to those with additional challenge, then he or she has the option of assigning a more appropriate prompt to these students.) Students first take 2 minutes to write down their response to the question. They then pair with a nearby partner who has selected the same question. After the partner groups have 2 minutes to chat, the teacher then elicits responses from all students in a whole class setting. Because the questions and prompts address the same learning goals (albeit at different levels of cognitive demand) the whole class discussion should help connect the various questions and prompts.

For example, an English/language arts lesson aligned to CCSS.ELA–LITERACY .W.9–10.1a (see Figure 4.4) would require students to investigate written claims from a variety of sources. After the class examines a claim from a current newspaper article, the teacher asks students to pause, think, and write down some ideas in response to one of the following (unlabeled) questions:

- Predict what opponents would disagree with in this claim (DOK Level 2).

- Formulate responses by opponents to counter this claim (DOK Level 3).

After students spend an appropriate amount of time thinking and preparing their responses, they find a partner who answered the same question and compare answers, compiling a "master list" from each pair. The teacher then engages the full class in sharing of points of contention and counters to those debatable points.

FIGURE 4.4: STANDARDS-ALIGNED EXAMPLE QUESTIONS AND PROMPTS FOR EACH KNOWLEDGE LEVEL—ELA/LITERACY CCSS: GRADES 9–10

Standard:	
CCSS.ELA-LITERACY.W.9–10.1a	
Introduce precise claim(s), distinguish the claim(s) from alternate or opposing claims, and create an organization that establishes clear relationships among claim(s), counterclaims, reasons, and evidence.	
One: Recall (Who, What, When, Where, Why)	State a claim arguing for or against school uniforms.
Two: Skill/Concept	Collect and categorize evidence for and against your claim.
Three: Strategic Thinking	Critique the merits of your claim based on the evidence you collect.
Four: Extended Thinking	Develop an advertisement (in written form with visuals) in support of your claim, making sure to include the evidence for your claim and that of a counterclaim. Given all the evidence you present, your advertisement should still convince others that your claim is the correct one.

Alternatively, when the class examines a different claim, the teacher could pose the same two prompts but require students to pair with a classmate who responded to the prompt they did *not* choose. In this mixed setup, student pairs combine the points of contention generated by one partner and the opposing responses generated by the other. Using Think/Pair/Share in both these fashions provides a means of Flexible Grouping and fosters a sense of classroom community while ensuring that all students are challenged appropriately and asked to extend their thinking.

3. The Three-Person Interview (Based on The Three Step Interview, Kagan & Kagan, 2009): Students are grouped in threes based on similar readiness, and then given a task card with three appropriately challenging prompts or questions based on Webb's Depth of Knowledge framework. Once situated with their task card in hand, the group reads the first prompt or question and each student briefly records his or her thoughts. One student begins as the interviewer, who then records the thoughts of the other two group members. Once all ideas have been recorded, the interviewer amends his or her initial response based on the ideas presented by the other two students. This process is repeated until each student has served as the interviewer and all three questions or prompts have been explored. Upon completion, the groups summarize their responses on chart paper to share with the whole class.

The history prompts in Figure 4.5 provide appropriate questions for such a task. As a formative assessment, the social studies teacher collects discussion board posts or entrance card responses to the question, "How did Thomas Jefferson's idea of 'independence' reflect his background and experiences?" Groups of three are formed according to the complexity of cause-and-effect relationships they discuss in their formative assessment.

FIGURE 4.5: STANDARDS-ALIGNED EXAMPLE QUESTIONS AND PROMPTS FOR EACH KNOWLEDGE LEVEL—ELA/LITERACY CCSS: HISTORY AND SOCIAL STUDIES, GRADES 11–12

Standard:	
CCSS.ELA-LITERACY.RH.11–12.6 *Evaluate authors' differing points of view on the same historical event or issue by assessing the authors' claims, reasoning, and evidence.*	
One: Recall **(Who, What, When, Where, Why)**	What are 2 to 3 key biographical facts about Thomas Jefferson?
Two: Skill/Concept	How did these biographical facts influence his role in crafting the Declaration of Independence?
Three: Strategic Thinking	Assess the strength of the grievances stated against the King of England in the Declaration of Independence. If you were a colonist at the time, would that be enough evidence for you to support a movement toward independence? Why or why not?
Four: Extended Thinking	If you were tasked with writing a new Declaration of Independence for today's world, what three unalienable rights should we all have, and why are these so important today? Make sure to cite historical and factual evidence to support your claims. (*Note:* If you think they are the same as the originals—life, liberty, and the pursuit of happiness—make a case for how these apply to today's world.)

Those who discuss deep or "layered" cause-and-effect relationships interview each other around portions of the following DOK Level 3 and 4 questions:

- "If you were a colonist at the time, would the grievances be enough evidence for you to support a movement toward independence? Why or why not?"

- "If you were tasked with writing a new Declaration of Independence for today's world, what three unalienable rights should we all have, and why are these so important today? Make sure to cite historical and factual evidence to support your claims."

- "Make a case for how the notions of 'life, liberty, and the pursuit of happiness' are perceived in similar and different ways today from how they were perceived at the time the Declaration was written."

Those whose formative assessment responses were less nuanced are placed in groups of three to interview each other around the following prompts derived from the DOK Level 2 and 3 questions:

- "In what ways did Jefferson's background and experience influence his role in crafting the Declaration of Independence? Discuss at least three cause-and-effect relationships."

- "Assess the strength of the grievances stated against the King of England in the Declaration of Independence. Which were the strongest points, in your opinion? Which were the weakest? Why?"

- "If you were a colonist at the time, would that be enough evidence for you to support a movement toward independence? Why or why not?"

Following the interview, the entire class discusses the question that was common to all groups ("If you were a colonist at the time . . .") and makes a list of the strengths and weaknesses discussed by each of the groups. This full class closure step is necessary to bring all students together to focus on the historical thinking involved in the task *and* to celebrate the varying viewpoints represented in the classroom.

Questioning at Home

Teachers using a flipped instructional approach have several differentiated options when questioning students at home. As mentioned previously, it is important that teachers structure the at-home experiences so that students are mentally engaged while viewing recorded lectures or videos.

1. Discussion Posts: Through the use of various learning management systems (i.e., Blackboard or Edmodo), teachers can create threads for students to respond to before, during, and/or after they view at-home direct instruction content. These threads can be differentiated based on readiness using questions or prompts at different levels of Webb's Depth of Knowledge framework. For instance, a teacher might have one thread created at Level 2 and another created at Level 3. Using formative assessment evidence gathered in class earlier that day, the teacher might assign students to a particular prompt based on colors (yellow group/blue group) that correspond with the titles of the discussion threads (Level 2 thread/Level 3 thread). A second possible method teachers can use to assign differentiated questions at home is to provide each student with a Quick Response (QR) code that, once scanned, will take students directly to their readiness-appropriate questions (QR codes can be created here, among other sites: http://www.qrstuff.com/). Once students are grouped, the teacher can then provide the appropriate QR code to students either digitally or as a hard copy. Regardless of how threads are assigned, using differentiated prompts ensures that students are responding to appropriately challenging questions during at-home activities. Furthermore, the use of differentiated discussion posts provides students with the forum and opportunity to respectfully respond to their classmates' ideas—a method that facilitates social processing of content through a virtual platform.

2. Blogging: There are several free and easy-to-use sites where students can create and maintain their own blog. LiveJournal and KidBlog are among the most user-friendly available (for a more detailed list of blogging resources see Appendix A). These blogs can be used to keep nightly reflections on content presented to students at home. As with discussion posts, to differentiate for readiness on blogs, teachers could provide students with leveled prompts that accompany at-home content. A teacher might also allow students to self-select which prompts best meet their readiness needs. If this is the case, they should be watchful for appropriate student choices as noted in the Think/Pair/Share section earlier.

For example, differentiated blog post topics could be assigned to students who are learning about the systems of checks and balances in the U.S. Federal Government. During at-home content delivery, students in need of more challenge will complete blog prompts such as:

- Evaluate it: Is the system working? Why or Why Not?

- Identify and depict a situation in your life where having a system of checks and balances will help you be successful. Make sure to draw direct connections to the Federal Government's system.

Those students who aren't quite ready for that level of challenge yet will respond to one of the following:

- Diagram the key elements of the Federal Government's system of checks and balances. Use your creativity to represent how each piece interacts with the others.

- What might happen if one element of the system of checks and balances was removed? Cite specific evidence.

By adjusting the level of challenge that students tackle while blogging at home, teachers can meet their learners at appropriate entry points for growth. Another method to accomplish this goal is through the use of scaffolding.

DIFFERENTIATING FOR READINESS THROUGH SCAFFOLDING

Scaffolding is the action of reducing the cognitive load that students must grapple with when exploring new or old concepts. When scaffolding an assignment, teachers should first consider what their most ready learners are capable of, and then use scaffolding to lift all other students to the same learning outcomes. Instead of lowering the bar, teachers provide students with a boost to reach it. This section (1) explores several scaffolding strategies and (2) provides practical examples of how teachers can implement these in school and at home. As discussed in Chapter 1, it is important that teachers proactively plan to differentiate for readiness beyond simply expecting some students to watch videos multiple times, or to hit pause as they are watching. The strategies explored are

- Small Group Instruction and Modeling

- Targeted Practice

- Tiered Graphic Organizers

Small Group Instruction and Modeling

The Gradual Release of Responsibility instructional framework (Fisher & Frey, 2013) proposes that teachers should purposefully design instruction to release the responsibility of learning to the students when they are of sufficient readiness to receive this responsibility. This takes place in four stages: **I do** (the teacher models), **we do** (the teacher guides and interacts with students), **you do together** (students collaborate in small groups), and **you do alone** (students work independently). Because students often arrive at the final two stages at different times, teachers should consider the use of Small Group Instruction and Modeling during the "we do together" stage to provide additional scaffolding for students in need of that structure. Below are at home and at school examples of Small Group Instruction and Modeling.

Small Group Instruction and Modeling in High School Earth Science

Standard:

HS-ESS1–5

Evaluate evidence of the past and current movements of continental and oceanic crust and the theory of plate tectonics to explain the ages of crustal rocks.

At School: Students in a high school earth science class watched a brief lecture on plate tectonics the previous night. As they arrive in class, the teacher asks them to post an answer to the following entrance question on TodaysMeet, "How can the theory of plate tectonics be used to predict the ages of crustal rocks?" Based on student responses, the teacher realizes that there are five students who are not ready to work in small groups to complete an activity involving predictions about crustal rocks. The teacher releases responsibility to the rest of the class to start a small group assignment, but then pulls the five struggling students for some reteaching and additional modeling of the theory of plate tectonics. After some additional instruction, the teacher checks for understanding via discussion, and is confident that the remaining five students are ready to work on the predictions activity.

At Home: Toward the end of this unit, the teacher assigns a "Cause and Effect" graphic organizer to check for individual students' understanding of plate tectonics. In surveying the finished products, the teacher determines that eight students need additional modeling before they are ready to complete the summative assessment. The teacher selects several brief Khan Academy videos that provide additional modeling of plate tectonics (for an example, see http://www.khanacademy.org/science/ cosmology-and-astronomy/earth-history-topic/plate-techtonics/v/plate-tectonics-evidence-of-plate-movement). These students participate in an online discussion thread in which they are asked to indicate two important ideas they learned, and one question that still remains. In addition, students are required to respond to at least three of their fellow classmates' remaining questions to provide a social learning experience at home. The teacher then checks their responses to make sure that the additional modeling has prepared them for the upcoming summative assessment. Because the teacher maintains a flexible learning environment, students who do not need additional scaffolding are instead asked to, at home, watch the following TED Talk on the hidden world of the deep ocean (http://www.ted.com/talks/robert_ballard_on_exploring_the_oceans) and to identify and explain three connections to the class exploration of plate tectonics and continental and oceanic crust.

Targeted Practice

Because not all students grasp new concepts at the same rate, teachers often will need to consider scaffolding student learning through Targeted Practice. One key element of Targeted Practice is to closely monitor to the impact previous instructional strategies have had on student learning and adjust future instruction accordingly. As a principle, teachers should consider asking students to explore concepts through different means of input, practice, and reflection rather than repeating strategies that were initially ineffective. "More often than not, when students do not learn, they do not need 'more'; rather they need 'different'" (Hattie, 2012, p. 83).

Targeted Practice in Geometry

> **Standard:**
>
> *CCSS.MATH.CONTENT.HSG-GMD.A.3*
>
> *Use volume formulas for cylinders, pyramids, cones, and spheres to solve problems.*

At School: A Math teacher starts off a class with a Padlet post to determine what students retained from the direct instruction they viewed the previous night (a recorded demonstration on using volume formulas for pyramids and cones). The teacher then determines that there is one skill that many students in the class seem to be struggling with: using the correct formula for pyramids. The teacher has set aside 10 to 15 minutes of class time to provide students with practice on this skill using the Khan Academy website, which has practice problems available specific to this topic.

Students work until they get five correct in a row before they stop and begin working on their enrichment activity, which involves searching for pyramids and cones within the classroom and then solving for volume based on student-recorded measurements. Students who did not have any errors on the introductory check for understanding will work on the pyramid-cone enrichment activity during this entire portion of the lesson.

At Home: During class, students are participating in an individual whiteboard activity where they are solving problems for volume of pyramids and cones, and then holding up their responses for the teacher to see. While this is taking place, the teacher is taking notes of who is struggling with the problems and who seems to have a strong grasp of the content. The teacher assigns homework based on student need, similar to the Khan Academy activity above (in fact, the teacher could use this same method if homework can be done digitally). The teacher also uses Knowmia .com to record brief tutorials solving for the volume of pyramids and cones and makes these available for students who need additional support while practicing these problems (for more information on Knowmia.com and other tools for flipping instruction, see resources in Appendix A). Students who do not need additional practice at home are asked to research a career that requires effective use of the volume formula. They will briefly share their findings with the class the next day.

Tiered Graphic Organizers

Adding or removing structure is a quick way to adjust the level of challenge for certain students. What follows is an example of how this can be done with tiered graphic organizers, both at home and at school.

Tiered Graphic Organizers in High School English

> **Standard:**
>
> *CCSS.ELA-LITERACY.W.11.12.8*
>
> *Gather relevant information from multiple authoritative print and digital sources, using advanced searches effectively; assess the strengths and limitations of each source in terms of the task, purpose, and audience; integrate information into the text selectively to maintain the flow of ideas, avoiding plagiarism and overreliance on any one source and following a standard format for citation.*

At School: Based on the sophistication of students' written responses from the previous class, an English teacher provides the following graphic organizers to help students collect information from relevant sources that address cyberbullying. In the first organizer (Figure 4.6, on the next page), little scaffolding is provided, and the task is left relatively open-ended. In the second version (Figure 4.7, on the next page), the teacher has reduced the cognitive demand by providing two specific sources, as well as a limitation of one of the sources to model what is expected of students completing the organizer.

FIGURE 4.6: AT-SCHOOL HIGHER READINESS GRAPHIC ORGANIZER—ANALYZING SOURCES

Sources	Strengths	Limitations	Additional Information
Online Source:			
Print Source:			
Your Choice:			

FIGURE 4.7: AT-SCHOOL LOWER READINESS GRAPHIC ORGANIZER—ANALYZING SOURCES

Sources	Strengths	Limitations	Additional Information
www.stopbullying.gov			
New York Times Magazine Article: The Online Avengers		This is by an author who also wrote a book on this topic. Her book is referenced at the end. Could that influence the usefulness of her ideas?	
Your Choice:			

THE DIFFERENTIATED FLIPPED CLASSROOM

At Home: The teacher has assigned a video for the students to watch that addresses the different types of research sources and their various benefits and limitations. The teacher intends for the students to complete this activity prior to class because they will be using this information for a self-directed research assignment. The teacher provides students with a note-taking graphic organizer, including reflection questions (see Figure 4.8). For students who need additional structure, the teacher has provided students with supplemental questions to help guide their responses (see Figure 4.9).

The use of Small Group Instruction and Modeling, Targeted Practice, and Tiered Graphic Organizers can provide teachers with diverse opportunities to support student learning both at home and at school.

FIGURE 4.8: AT-HOME HIGHER READINESS GRAPHIC ORGANIZER—AUTHOR'S PURPOSE

Question:	Responses:
Which sources are best when your goal is to inform? Persuade?	
Why should authors consider their audience when writing?	

FIGURE 4.9: AT-HOME LOWER READINESS GRAPHIC ORGANIZER—AUTHOR'S PURPOSE

Question:	Responses:
Which sources are best to use when your goal is to inform? Persuade?	Consider: • Where can we find relatively unbiased information? • List some of the sources you go to for factual information. • How are these different from those you might use to persuade someone? • List those sources as well.
Why should authors consider their audience when writing?	Consider: • How does your writing change when you are e-mailing a friend versus a teacher? • What does this say about the impact of the audience when writing?

DIFFERENTIATING FOR READINESS THROUGH VARIED CONTENT DELIVERY

The techniques discussed thus far present approaches to differentiating the *process* through which students interact with content to meet varying readiness needs. Students approach the same content and learning goals, albeit with different tools and structures that provide various levels of support and challenge. It is also possible to differentiate for readiness by adjusting the accessibility or challenge of the *content* itself. In the following section, we explore how providing varied levels of **texts** and **videos** can accomplish this goal. (*Note:* It is also possible to differentiate *products*; we explore this method regarding student choice in Chapter 5.)

Varied Levels of Texts

Any teacher who asks a classroom full of students to interact with text comes face to face with the harsh reality that just because they are in the same grade doesn't mean they are all on the same reading level. There are several digital resources that can help address this issue. Both Newsela.com and Commonlit.org are free resources that offer texts on various reading and Lexile levels.

Newsela.com, as its name suggests, is a storehouse of recent news articles on curricular topics such as science, health, art, and social studies, as well as areas of general categories, such as kids and sports. Every article featured is offered in five different reading levels spanning Grade 3 through Grade 12. Some articles are accessible in Spanish as well. This allows a teacher to easily assign the same article to all students while ensuring they can access it at their reading level. There are several options for doing so, such as assigning the whole class a general grade level and then helping students adjust that level so that the task better "fits" them. Newsela, an adaptive website, also offers a feature that tracks student performance and reports student levels and progress to the teacher.

Commonlit.org operates a little differently. The site offers a collection of different texts all clustered around a similar theme. Texts vary by Lexile and grade level (usually from fifth-grade to twelfth-grade level) as well as by genre (short stories, poems, news, ads, etc.). A teacher using this resource begins by selecting a theme to explore with the class, such as *Resilience, America, Fear and Paranoia,* or *Friendship and Loyalty*. Within that theme, there are several discussion questions from which to choose. For instance, a teacher wishing to conduct an exploration of the theme *Resilience* might choose the discussion question, "How does a person overcome adversity?" To differentiate based on readiness, the teacher could assign a nonfiction piece about Bethany Hamilton (the champion surfer who survived a shark attack) to students reading on grade level. Those who need more support may be assigned a news article on Yul Kwon (a survivor of bullying turned reality-television star/*Survivor* contestant). Although the Kwon piece is slightly below grade level, it offers an equally respectful and intriguing perspective. Each piece features discussion questions at the end;

however, a more powerful way to unite readers and build community as examined in Chapter 2 would be to ask everyone to answer the discussion question ("How does a person overcome adversity?") from the perspective of the person they read about (including textual support). Students could post their responses on one of the back-channel sites described in Appendix A (e.g., TodaysMeet). Alternatively, teachers could allow students to pick from several poems featured in a grade category (e.g., seventh or eighth) and assign them tiered graphic organizers to support their process. It's probably a good idea to use both approaches during a unit or semester so that students can work with both similar and different genres.

For both sites, it may be a good idea to allow students to access and process the readings in class, at first, and post their discussion responses at home perhaps after viewing some supporting content. Once students get used to the sites, they can access them at home, opening up more flexibility for teachers. Because the texts are (a) engaging and (b) the right reading "fit" for students, the possibilities are endless for opportunities for reading and processing opportunities both at home and at school.

Varied Levels of Videos

Videos offer yet another form of content that can be differentiated to meet students' varying readiness needs. As detailed in Appendix A, there are numerous sites that offer ready-made videos (e.g., YouTube and Khan Academy) as well as resources that allow teachers to personalize videos with their own questions or prompts (e.g., edu-Canon and Zaption). Teachers can use both types of resources to differentiate for readiness. If using ready-made videos, teachers might select and assign two videos to different groups of students: one that offers challenge by explaining a topic more abstractly or in greater depth, and another that provides more support through a more concrete or accessible presentation of content.

The example in Figure 4.10 shows how a fourth-grade teacher might use videos to differentiate for readiness after a formative assessment revealed that some of her students were ready for an additional layer of challenge, while others were still making basic errors distinguishing among parallel, intersecting, and perpendicular lines. This example aligns with CCSS.MATH.CONTENT.4.G.A.1: *Draw points, lines, line segments, rays, angles (right, acute, obtuse), and perpendicular and parallel lines. Identify these in two-dimensional figures.*

If ready-made videos are not as tightly aligned to learning goals as a teacher would like, he or she could instead personalize videos by to meet students' varying readiness needs by modifying the questions used during those videos. Webb's DOK framework (2002)—outlined earlier in the chapter—provides one method of doing so. A second way to differentiate content based on readiness would be to add in frequent key summary points to videos that would essentially act as scaffolding for students as they viewed the content. This would be similar to highlighting text to draw students' attention to the key points.

FIGURE 4.10: DIFFERENTIATING READY-MADE VIDEO CONTENT BASED ON READINESS

| Video 1 | For additional challenge, the students who showed no errors on the most recent formative assessment will extend their exploration of lines and angles to solving for "mystery angles": https://www.khanacademy.org/math/basic-geo/basic-geo-angles/basic-geo-interpreting-angles/v/decomposing-angles

Although this video introduces some new ideas, if accompanied by the proper guiding questions (e.g., "What connections can you make between this and what we discussed in class?") and social processing, students will be stretched to transfer their understanding of lines and angles to a new context. |
|---|---|
| Video 2 | For those students who need some additional support distinguishing between perpendicular, parallel, and intersecting lines, the teacher could share the following video from Khan Academy that takes a direct and concrete approach to reviewing this concept:https://www.khanacademy.org/math/basic-geo/basic-geo-angles/basic-geo-interpreting-angles/v/identifying-parallel-and-perpendicular-lines

After reviewing the video and answering the accompanying questions, the students return to the previous lesson's formative assessment to see if they have grasped the content with which they originally struggled. |

The following example illustrates how a ninth-grade teacher might differentiate by scaffolding a video with key summary points. In this example, the teacher first gathered formative assessment data on students' readiness to infer the meaning of key vocabulary words in primary documents. Since the class was learning about the Civil War, the teacher based this assignment on the Gettysburg Address and aligned the lesson with CCSS.ELA-LITERACY.RH.9-10.4: *Determine the meaning of words and phrases as they are used in a text, including vocabulary describing political, social, or economic aspects of history/social science.* Figure 4.11 shows how this teacher differentiated content based on readiness for this activity by personalizing the video.

As is illustrated by the use of graphic organizers in this example, teachers could (and should) use any of the active processing strategies presented throughout this book to accompany tiered texts and videos.

A process-approach combined with a content-approach to readiness differentiation provides teachers with different ways to personalize learning for all students, regardless of their learning needs.

FIGURE 4.11: DIFFERENTIATING PERSONALIZED VIDEO CONTENT BASED ON READINESS

The teacher used the following video of a reading of the Gettysburg Address: https://www.youtube.com/watch?v=BvA0J_2ZpIQ	
Students who did not need additional support—as determined by the formative assessment—were provided with the video link and a graphic organizer that asked them to identify challenging vocabulary, as well as to infer the meaning of those challenging words based on the context of how they were used in the video.	For students who struggled on the formative assessment and needed additional scaffolding, the teacher personalized the video by pausing each time key vocabulary word was used (e.g., *consecrated, hallow, conceived*) and inserting clues as to the meaning of the words. Students used the clues provided to identify the meaning of key words on their graphic organizers.

A NOTE ON FLEXIBLE GROUPING

We briefly want to return to the concept of Flexible Grouping here. For illustrative purposes, many of the readiness examples included in this chapter are for same-readiness groups of students. This is an important practice in a differentiated classroom—or any classroom, for that matter. In a comprehensive review of research on grouping and student achievement, Hattie (2012) notes that including small group learning activities with the appropriate materials/tasks for each group produces a positive effect on student achievement (0.49). However, it is important to note that mixed-readiness groupings should be implemented regularly. Hattie (2012) also notes that cooperative learning has a greater effect on student achievement than individualistic learning due to the impact of working with peers. From a human standpoint, it makes sense that opportunities for group work should come in different forms so that students become aware of the various ways their peers learn and come to recognize challenge as universal to struggling and more advanced learners alike. As mentioned in Chapter 2, the notion that students benefit from interacting with peers in different capacities is a hallmark of Flexible Grouping, a key principle of a differentiated classroom that involves employing various grouping strategies based on different elements of student learning (Tomlinson, 2003). Regarding student readiness, it is beneficial to have students work in mixed-readiness groups as well as same-readiness groups to maximize the academic and social benefits of peer interactions. Chapter 5 examines how to group students based on other elements of their learning—interest and learning profile—and discusses how these grouping configurations can help facilitate Flexible Grouping.

THE BOTTOM LINE

Differentiating according to student readiness—both at home and at school—is necessary to making sure all students progress. As Hattie (2012) reminds us, the teacher's role is to move every student forward "+1" his or her learning. Since students do not come to us at the same stage of readiness, the same instruction will fail to move them all forward. This chapter has discussed strategies for providing students with the necessary degree of support and challenge needed for them to grow, both at home and at school.

A TEACHER IN ACTION

As Ms. Velazquez continued to gather formative assessment data through various measures (see Chapter 3), she began to see more clearly exactly what students needed to move forward in their learning. She continued to use Team Huddles, but became savvier about what students—both in and out of the huddles—worked on during those discussions. If she huddled with students who were having difficulty, she provided the rest of the class with questions at Levels 3 and 4 of Webb's Depth of Knowledge—such as those listed in Figure 4.2 on page 42—to work on in pairs or small groups. Conversely, if she needed to huddle with a small group of students who needed additional challenge, she could provide them with a DOK Level 3 or 4 question to crunch on to push their thinking while the rest of the class wrestled with the concepts that the small "down the road" group had already mastered.

One of Ms. Velazquez's biggest points of growth, however, came from discovering ways to differentiate when the Team Huddle just wasn't enough. There were times when the class was split regarding readiness, and pulling just one small group wasn't sufficient to meet students' needs. In these instances, she began using the Three-Person Interview Model to tier the challenge level of the questions and problems students wrestled with in class. She could monitor group work easily this way and bring everyone together using a question that was common to all groups. In addition, she noticed this technique was pushing all students to "construct viable arguments and critique the reasoning of others"—a key standard for mathematical practice in the Common Core State Standards (CCSS.MATH.PRACTICE.MP3).

Increasingly, Tiered Graphic Organizers became a key tool for Ms. Velazquez, as did Tiered Online Resources from Khan Academy, TEDEd (ed.ted.com), and so on. Often, all students used the same graphic organizer (e.g., those presented in Chapter 3), albeit in response to different videos that addressed the same concept with varying degrees of complexity. This helped ensure accountability and helped everyone feel that they were all moving forward together, even if they occasionally took different routes to get there.

But as the school year came to an end, Ms. Velazquez couldn't help but notice that some students had consistently required additional support from her and some students had consistently needed additional challenge. She had worked in mixed-readiness and random groupings as often possible to make sure her groups were flexible, but she wondered how she could strategically and purposefully group students according to a commonality other than readiness. She knew her students received the necessary support and challenge from her regarding their readiness needs, but a part of her wanted to mix it up just a little bit more the following year.

CHAPTER 5

Differentiating According to Student Interest and Learning Profile

I like having choice. I would say that it helps me and it helps other students learn more.

—Ninth Grader

You definitely have a wide variety of assignments you can choose from, and that helps to make it more fun for you to learn.

—Tenth Grader

It gets rid of that attitude of, "Oh, I don't want to do this; I don't like doing this stuff; it's not fun." It makes it so the work's less stressful too, so that's another positive.

—Twelfth Grader

The students quoted above had teachers who routinely offered them options for how they took in, processed, and demonstrated their learning (Doubet, 2007, p. 234). Their responses illuminate the motivating power of choice. They also remind us that—in differentiated classrooms—*readiness* is not the only aspect of student learning that needs attention; *interest* and *learning profile* must also be considered (Sousa & Tomlinson, 2011).

MOTIVATION IN A FLIPPED CLASSROOM

Too often, educators adopt a *Field of Dreams* mentality regarding the use of technology in the classroom: "If we have it, they will learn." This perception is in large part fueled by the misconception of the nature of students' interactions with technology outside school. Students do spend a large amount of time with technology (Project Tomorrow, 2013; Salaway, Caruso, & Nelson, 2007); however, while students are "plugged in," they are most likely communicating with friends, exploring areas of interest, and sharing opinions about relevant topics. In other words, it isn't just the *technology itself* that appeals to students; it is technology's role as a vehicle to *connect students to what matters to them* that leads to its prolific use.

Likewise, if educators exploring a flipped approach to instruction wish to motivate students, simply asking them to use a gadget will not suffice; rather, teachers must strive to (1) discover what matters to students, (2) create learning opportunities that connect students to these important aspects of their lives, (3) give students choice/power over *how* they learn, and (4) find ways to use technology as a tool to facilitate these opportunities. Such opportunities for connection and choice can provide students with the "intrinsic motivation" that is of vital importance for student success in a flipped classroom. Both brain research (e.g., Jensen, 2005; Willis, 2006) and educational research (e.g., Bransford, Brown, & Cocking, 2000) reveal that students perform better when they see some *connection* between the content and themselves and/or the world around them.

By finding avenues to reveal such connections, we have a better chance of harnessing student attention and investment, particularly when asking students to participate in direct instruction away from school. Brain research also reveals that *novelty* plays an important role in attention and motivation (e.g., Perry, 2000; Willis, 2007). Our brains naturally "perk up" when met with something unusual. Allowing students to approach a topic in a unique manner—or through an avenue they have chosen—can increase student alertness; as a result, they may attend to and retain material more efficiently than they would have otherwise.

> If educators exploring a flipped approach to instruction wish to motivate students, simply asking them to use a gadget will not suffice.

This chapter explores tools for discovering and harnessing student interests—both at home and at school—as a means of motivating students and improving their learning. It also presents several strategies for providing students with choices in how they take in, process, and showcase required information and skills. Such strategies not only serve to personalize learning for students, but they also help facilitate Flexible Grouping—another vital component of a differentiated flipped classroom.

GETTING ON THE SAME PAGE: INTEREST AND LEARNING PROFILE

The idea of adjusting instruction for student "readiness" has been discussed at length in Chapters 3 and 4, but what does it mean to differentiate according to student "interest" and "learning profile"? If 20 different educators were asked that question, they might respond with 20 very different answers! Rather than explore the myriad definitions and conceptions that exist, this brief summary outlines those that most closely apply to the strategies presented in this chapter.

Student Interest

Harnessing student interest, at its most basic level, means designing assignments that connect students with "those topics or pursuits that evoke [their] curiosity and passion" (Tomlinson, 2003, p. 3). Appealing to student interest certainly goes a long way toward personalizing their learning experience. There are two different kinds of student interest—personal and situational—that can help teachers do so (Schraw, Flowerday, & Lehman, 2001).

- *Personal interests* are those students bring with them into the classroom. They are activated internally and hold "enduring personal value" (Schraw et al., 2001, p. 211). For example, a student may be passionate about skateboarding, fascinated with filmmaking, or intensely curious about traveling to other parts of the world. When we find ways to connect content with the things students are already excited about, we are tapping into their personal interests.

- *Situational interests*, on the other hand, arise more spontaneously. They can be activated in a particular situation in response to a certain context or environment (i.e., a class or a lesson). Anytime we present students with several options for an assignment and allow them to choose the one that is most appealing, we are harnessing the power of situational interest.

Ideally, to engage the largest range of students in our lessons both at home and at school, we will appeal to both personal and situational interests.

Learning Profile

While we can classify interests into two categories, defining "learning profile" is a bit more complex. Anyone who has spent time with a group of students knows that they differ vastly in their reactions to various modes of instruction, respond to authority in different fashions, and operate more efficiently in a variety of environments (e.g., noise levels, amounts of movement, grouping configurations). All of these factors fall under the umbrella of "learning profile" (Tomlinson, 2014). While teachers should absolutely be aware of these differences and provide instruction through varying modes and in flexible environments, there is little research to support the practice of "diagnosing" students with different learning style labels and assigning work accordingly (Hattie & Yates, 2014). This holds true for *intelligence preferences* as well—another trait that falls under the learning profile umbrella. Theorists such as Gardner (1995, 2006) and Sternberg and Grigorenko (2007) provide frameworks for thinking about intelligence preferences—or how students best take in, process, and produce knowledge. But even Gardner and Sternberg stress the contextual nature of such choices and advise against labeling students with specific styles and assigning choices accordingly. Sound practice regarding differentiation, then, would involve (1) creating several task options aligned to *different intelligence preferences* but the *same learning goals* and (2) allowing students to *choose* the task that seems to fit them best. It is also important that teachers design such task options to focus on *student thinking* rather than on a particular kind of *product*. Because of the potential to use intelligence preferences to create assignment *options*, or *choices*, this chapter discusses learning profile—specifically, Robert Sternberg's Triarchic Framework—as another means of activating students' *situational interests* (those arising in response to a certain context or environment). Learning profile options also present students with novel approaches to content—a practice that brain researchers recommend for piquing interest and activating attention (e.g., Willis, 2007).

Discovering and Responding to Personal Interests

Personal interests are those that drive inquiry and debate. They can capture students' imaginations and help them focus for long periods of time (Csikszentmihalyi, 1990). They draw students into learning and assist them in seeing that what they are studying is connected to who they are as people. It is impossible for teachers to harness these interests, however, if they are not aware of them. Therefore, teachers in differentiated flipped classrooms take active steps to discover what makes their students come alive in the world outside the classroom. Any of the strategies discussed in Chapter 2 (e.g., "ME" Post Cards, Google Forms) can help teachers discover students' personal affinities and interests, since part of creating a classroom community is knowing the students within that community. Another technique is to strategically collect information on students' interests while asking them to reflect on how those hobbies, curiosities, and passions might connect to classroom content (see Figure 5.1).

> Teachers in differentiated flipped classrooms take active steps to discover what makes their students come alive in the world outside the classroom.

FIGURE 5.1: INTEREST CARDS

Directions: I'd really like to know what you are excited about so that I can connect those areas of interest to some of the assignments and examples I use in class. In each box below, please indicate an interest of yours and describe briefly how you are involved with that interest. Please also brainstorm some ways that this interest might connect with our class's content.

Name:	Name:
Interest #1:	Interest #2:
Experience with it?	Experience with it?
Connection with this subject?	Connection with this subject?

SOURCE: Tomlinson (2005).

While such formal measures are important, informal observation can be powerful as well. Just by spending time talking to students in an authentic manner, teachers can find areas of general interest that might serve to hook all students into expending more effort on their tasks. For example, English teacher Katie Carson noticed that one of her reluctant writers wore football jerseys to school on a regular basis. She harnessed that opportunity by suggesting he describe the game of football to her—the rules, plays, strategies, and so on—in his journal during free-write time. She explained that she desperately wanted to seem informed about football when she watched games with her friends on Sundays, so it would be a win-win for them both. That simple suggestion transformed a student who habitually submitted blank pages into a writer who filled the pages of his journal with diagrams and lengthy prose explanations (Tomlinson & Doubet, 2005). Instructional decisions like this one would translate seamlessly to a flipped environment with the use of student journals and blogs kept online.

SIMPLE STRATEGIES FOR HARNESSING STUDENTS' PERSONAL INTERESTS

Katie Carson's use of journal writing illustrates a natural, responsive approach to making learning relevant for students. But to truly harness the motivational power of student interests, *planning ahead* is key. Once teachers take steps to discover what their students are interested in, there are several low-prep, proactive steps they can employ to naturally weave students' personal interests into the fabric of required course content, both at home and at school.

At Home

As discussed in Chapter 3, online discussion posts can provide formative assessment information that reveals students' grasp of at-home content-delivery. Structuring brief, at-home processing to direct instruction based on student interest compliments the readiness strategies suggested in Chapter 4. With a little bit of adjusting, the same discussion posts strategy (journal prompts, story problems, etc.) can be differentiated to reflect students' hobbies, activities, and curiosities. In fact, recent studies (e.g., Walkington, 2013) have discovered that algebra students who were given problems contextualized to their out-of-school interests (e.g., sports, movies, music, food) solved problems faster and more accurately than did students who received traditional story algebra problems (see Figure 5.2).

Although the adjustments to such problems are seemingly minor, they can make a significant difference in student investment and performance (Walkington, 2013). Even more promising, those students who worked with the Interest-Based Problems *grew more* in their efficiency and accuracy—even when the "treatment" was removed—than did the students who received traditional problems. In other words,

FIGURE 5.2: MATH CCSS–ALIGNED SAMPLE TRADITIONAL STORY PROBLEM ADJUSTED TO MATCH STUDENT INTERESTS

Standard:

CCSS.MATH.CONTENT.6.SP.B.5.C

Giving quantitative measures of center (median and/or mean) and variability (interquartile range and/or mean absolute deviation), as well as describing any overall pattern and any striking deviations from the overall pattern with reference to the context in which the data were gathered.

Interest	Problem Text
Traditional	A sample of ten middle school students was asked to count the number of writing utensils that they own. Student responses are represented in the following set of numbers: 5, 4, 2, 10, 6, 14, 8, 5, 1, 8 • What is average of the set numbers? • What is the median of the set of numbers? • Create a "five-number summary" of the data and display it in boxplot format • What patterns do you see in the data?
Video Games	Ten middle school students whom play video games were asked how many hours they spend playing each week. Their responses are represented in the following set of numbers: 5, 4, 2, 10, 6, 14, 8, 5, 1, 8 [same questions as traditional problem]
Social Media	Ten middle school students that use Facebook were asked how many status updates they post each week. Their responses are represented in the following set of numbers: 5, 4, 2, 10, 6, 14, 8, 5, 1, 8 [same questions as traditional problem]
Sports	The basketball coach was frustrated with the amount of players fouling out. For the next five games, the coach kept a record of every time a player committed a foul. The numbers below represent each player's total amount of fouls over a five-game period. 5, 4, 2, 10, 6, 14, 8, 5, 1, 8 [same questions as traditional problem]

SOURCE: Used with permission of Stephen Caviness.

interest differentiation can act "as a scaffold, providing grounding for students as they learn important skills relating to coordinating situation and problem models when writing algebraic expressions" (Walkington, 2013, p. 942). Findings such as these suggest that attending to student interests may not simply be a nicety as much as a necessity for student growth.

At School

For a low-prep way to incorporate interest differentiation into at-school instruction, we can return to the "Four Corners" activity described in Chapter 2 (pages 16–17). This strategy can be adapted to increase motivation by infusing student pastimes into the choices offered in the four corners. For example, an English teacher might ask students to view three ads of interest to them on YouTube the night before and post in their journals (1) the products advertised in these ads and (2) why they chose those products. The teacher surveys the journal posts to determine what kinds of products seem most interesting to students (potential product categories are shown below). In class the following day, the teacher would assign four corners based on the subject of those ads and tell students to move to the corner that represents what they would *most* like to study as part of a unit on argument:

- **Corner 1:** Ads for phones, tablets, or laptops

- **Corner 2:** Ads for beauty products endorsed by popular recording artists

- **Corner 3:** Ads for sports drinks endorsed by famous athletes

- **Corner 4:** Ads for video gaming systems

Once students arrive at their chosen corner, they find a combination of additional print and digital ads (bookmarked on laptops or tablets) that they must analyze and evaluate according to designated criteria. Corner groups subdivide into smaller groups of three or four students, if necessary, and each student must emerge from group time with a completed graphic organizer that captures the claims, evidence, reasoning, and logical fallacies included each ad as well as a rating of its effectiveness and suggestions for improvement. In this way, the class can converge as a whole to discuss the same understandings, knowledge, and skills, albeit through examples that are important to students.

A common misconception is that personal interests can be accessed only through long-term projects or inquiry-driven units. But the examples above demonstrate that teachers can connect classroom content to the real-world topics, people, and situations their students care about, even in everyday instruction. Granted, such connections are not always possible; when they are not, tasks designed to evoke "situational interest" can provide an alternative approach to increasing student motivation, both at home and at school.

STRATEGIES FOR ACTIVATING STUDENTS' SITUATIONAL INTERESTS

Unlike personal interests, situational interests are not so much about students' inherent interest in a topic as about the power to choose. The autonomy students experience when they have some control over how they learn serves as a motivator—especially for students who are typically disengaged (Schraw et al., 2001). Furthermore, well-designed task options can serve as motivators because they present some degree of novelty—something different from the typical school fare. But what is involved in creating "well-designed task options"? First, all tasks must lead students toward the same learning goals; *alignment* is key. Second, the options must *vary* enough to be intriguing to a range of students but *similar* enough that they can be discussed as a full class after completion. Differentiation is not just about different tasks, but about different tasks that lead to the *same outcomes*; thus, both structure and planning are required for successful implementation. Further, the student-centered nature of classroom instruction facilitated by a flipped approach is rife with opportunities to capitalize on student interest.

> Situational interests are not so much about students' inherent interest in a topic as about the power to choose.

The following section presents four frameworks designed to help teachers create task options. *Jigsaw*, *RAFT*, *Learning Menus*, and *TriMind* are all designed to (1) appeal to students' situational interests, (2) align to important learning goals, and (3) encourage Flexible Grouping and full group sharing at their completion.

Jigsaw

Jigsaw is a cooperative learning strategy originally developed by Aronson and Patnoe (1997). In a Jigsaw assignment, different groups serve as "experts" for different pieces of a content puzzle. When representatives from each of the expert groups return to their home groups to share their piece of the puzzle, the full picture emerges. The motivational power of situational interest is activated when students are allowed to choose the piece of the puzzle in which they want to become an expert. Specifically, the steps of a Jigsaw include:

1. "Home Groups" of four to five students meet and select the options they'd most like to study (home group size corresponds to the number of topic options available).

2. Students regroup into "Expert Groups" with students who chose the same options (*Note:* Jigsaw can also be used as a form of readiness differentiation, with the teacher *assigning* the expert groups according to complexity of material rather than asking students to *choose* their expert groups).

3. Expert Groups complete a structured activity to research, read about, or study their chosen topic; they must emerge with concrete information to share with their Home Groups

4. Students return to Home Groups and share their findings/work. Home Group members complete a graphic organizer or other structured activity to capture information presented by their classmates. They also complete a synthesis task to pull all the different "pieces of the puzzle" together.

5. Full class discussion may ensue, followed by checks for understanding at both group and individual levels.

Ms. O'Brien used a Jigsaw to divide and conquer the different types of problems involving polynomials, requiring students to teach the others in their home group how to solve their chosen types of problems. She put students into home groups of four to review the terms *monomial and polynomial*. She then described four different types of polynomial problems and instructed each home group to "divide and conquer" by allowing group members to choose the type of problem they wanted to learn more about. Students regrouped into "expert groups" with those who had chosen the same type of problem and studied the problem using varied resources (textbook investigation, Khan Academy viewing, and discussion). Ms. O'Brien monitored expert group work closely to answer questions and clear up misconceptions. When expert groups finished, students returned to their home groups to explain their problem type to their group members; this was followed by group discussion and several checks for understanding. Ms. O'Brien built structure, progress monitoring, and accountability into each step of the Jigsaw to ensure attention and success (see Appendix C.1 for more specifics).

Jigsaw can be used exclusively at school or as an at-home/at-school hybrid. In Ms. O'Brien's case, the expert group work could have been tackled at home with students collaborating in online forums while watching select content in their "at-home" expert groups. These online forums and checks for understanding can be conducted via digital means (e.g., Padlet, backchannels, Google Doc). In either case, accountability is key, but the added motivation provided by students choosing their topics makes such accountability checks feel more like "sharing" and less like "monitoring." An additional benefit of Jigsaw is that it supplies a structure for Flexible Grouping, because students must work in two different grouping configurations—whether online or in class—to complete the activity.

RAFT

A RAFT (Buehl, 2009; Santa, 1988) asks students to take on a Role, address a specified Audience in an appropriate Format about a particular Topic. Student interest can be piqued simply by the novelty of this approach; however, the teacher can tap into situational interest by designing several different options for Role, Audience, Format, and Topic—all crafted to address the same learning goals (see Figure 5.3).

By allowing students to select the combination or "row" that intrigues them most, teachers are more likely to amplify student investment. They can also build in opportunities for Flexible Grouping because students can work with others who have chosen the same row to construct responses or products, and then meet with students who selected different options to share results.

FIGURE 5.3: **RAFT OPTION TEMPLATE**

Role	Audience	Format	Topic

FIGURE 5.4: **ELA GRAMMAR RAFT**

Standard:

CCSS.ELA-LITERACY.L.8.2

Demonstrate command of the conventions of Standard English capitalization, punctuation, and spelling when writing.

Role	Audience	Format	Topic
Semicolon	Comma and Conjunction	Blog post using both forms of punctuation (semicolon and common/conjunction)	"The two of you are needy; I don't need anyone but me."
Comma	Conjunction	Series of reconciliatory Facebook posts using both forms of punctuation (semicolon and common/conjunction)	"I'm sorry! I can't do my sentence-separation job without you!"
Semicolon, Comma, and Conjunction	Middle School Students	Series of "sidebar" sponsoring ads—at least one ad from each of the three roles (semicolon, comma, conjunction). Use all three tools in your ads.	"I'm the best tool for the job!"

A middle school language arts teacher used the RAFT in Figure 5.4 as a follow-up to an online tutorial she had created for students to watch for homework the night before. They were to take notes on each method of fixing run-on sentences while they viewed; they used those notes during the following class period as resources for completing the RAFT option that most appealed to them.

Each option allowed students to demonstrate what they understood about sentence combination and the tools used to accomplish that purpose. To encourage Flexible Grouping, the teacher allowed students to work with classmates who chose the same option they did. Following completion, each group shared their products with the class, and the teacher used those responses to guide further instruction and correct misconceptions.

A science teacher used the RAFT in Figure 5.5 to motivate students to follow through on lab safety. He added the "Points of Discussion" column to ensure that students included all necessary information.

Students worked in groups of two to four on the row of their choice, and then got into mixed groups to share their responses; in this way, the RAFT was used as a modified Jigsaw activity (and thus facilitated Flexible Grouping). As expert groups presented, their classmates took notes on the graphic organizer provided by their teacher, which served as review material for the Lab Safety test. The products generated by the groups (e.g., wanted posters, magazine spreads) were displayed in the room to serve as tangible reminders of proper lab behavior.

While the two RAFT examples displayed in Figures 5.4 and 5.5 were used as formative assessment checks, RAFTs can also be used in a more summative fashion, calling on students to complete work both at home and at school. If they use RAFTs in this manner, teachers must be sure to include detailed task directions—along with clear rubrics—to ensure that all options are aligned to the same learning goals and that students will know exactly what is expected of them to be successful. Appendix C.2 has examples of more developed RAFTs suitable for use as summative assessments.

In a flipped classroom, teachers might also consider assigning "Pre-RAFT" at-home content to prepare students for work on their selected RAFT during class the following day. For example, the middle school teacher who developed the Language Arts Grammar RAFT in Figure 5.4 could assign students the tutorial at the following site: http://data.grammarbook.com/blog/commas/connecting-sentences-with-commas-and-semicolons/ and ask them to take the quiz that follows. The next day would begin with a brief discussion of insights and questions raised by the tutorial/quiz before moving on to the RAFT activity.

FIGURE 5.5: LAB SAFETY RAFT

Role	Audience	Format	Topic	Points of Discussion
Teen Magazine's Fashion Editor	Middle School Students	Double-Page Magazine Spread	"Wear What's 'IN' in Science Lab Fashion"	Eyewear; ear-wear; long hair; baggy clothes; jewelry; long sleeves
Referee	Science "Lab-thletes"	Instruction Playbook	"Instant Replay Out-takes: Avoid Fouls in the Science Lab"	Running; horseplay; injuries; anchor activities
The Science Lab	The Public	Wanted Posters	"Wanted: Students Caught in the Act of Breaking Cleanup Laws"	Your three primary "cleanup" responsibilities; your work area
Newspaper Writer	Readers of Our Local Paper	Exposé Cover Story	"Undercover in the Science Lab: Why Lab Materials Are About to Protest"	Proper handling of chemicals, beakers, other materials; cabinet arrangement

SOURCE: Adapted from Doubet in Strickland (2007).

NOTE: The NGSS do *not* address lab safety; rather, their developers recommend utilizing state lab safety standards.

Learning Menus

Learning Menus (Cummings, 2000) are designed to motivate students through offering several "courses" of choices. They function much like limited "restaurant week" menus that seek to showcase a restaurant's specialty dishes by presenting diners with a few dishes from which to select in each course. Similarly, in a Learning Menu, students are presented with a few options in different categories (main courses, side dishes, desserts) and encouraged to design the "meal" combination that offers the most appealing manner by which to "digest" the unit's specific learning goals. Specific steps for designing a Learning Menu are as follows:

1. Articulate your standards and aligned learning goals for the menu.

2. Decide which learning goals you want to address in each "course."

3. Begin by designing one or more **Appetizers**, which are opening activities that can serve as "hooks" for the menu. They may be introductory videos, readings, or tasks (e.g., interviews) that will get students thinking about the ideas they'll "chew on" for the rest of the unit.

4. Create your **Main Dishes** by identifying tasks that you want all students to complete. The main dishes section could look the same for every student in the class. (*Note:* If you want to infuse *readiness* differentiation, you could create more than one version of the Learning Menu with different main-dish tasks on each version.) Student must complete all the main-dish items on their assigned learning menu. Each "dish" should be clearly tied to the key learning objectives.

5. Design several **Side Dishes** to tackle learning goals not yet addressed in the main dishes. Students should select a specified number of side dishes (e.g., select 2 from a list of 4) and complete the side-dish options that appeal to them most. It is important to make sure that *all* side dishes address the same learning goals so that no matter which options students choose, they will get the same "nutrients." Side-dish options may also be aligned to intelligence preferences (see TriMind section on page 74).

6. Design several **Dessert** tasks that students will be very motivated to complete (in other words, we should not have to persuade students to "eat their dessert!").

   • Desserts should be appealing, engaging tasks that—at best—tap into students' personal interests in relation to the topic.

   • Desserts can be optional activities that only some students choose to complete, or there might be an expectation that all students will complete at least one.

   • In some cases it might be appropriate for students to devise their own desserts.

7. Designate which aspects of the menu should be completed at home, which aspects should be completed at school, and which aspects can be completed in either setting.

8. Gather and bookmark all necessary URLs so that students can access them easily both at home and at school.

Mr. Sager used a Learning Menu in each of his major mathematics units as means of allowing students to see math at work in the real world. For each unit, he attempted to tap into something he recognized as a common interest of his students (e.g., ice

FIGURE 5.6: MATH LEARNING MENU

Standard:

CCSS.MATH.CONTENT.HSF.LE.A.2

Construct linear and exponential functions, including arithmetic and geometric sequences, given a graph, a description of a relationship, or two input-output pairs.

Radioactive Ice Cream Menu

Main Dish (complete all)

- Define what a logarithm and exponential are and what they are used for

- All of a sudden there are no more supplies for making ice cream. The world now has 5,000,000 bowls of ice cream left. 22% of this ice cream is being consumed every minute. How long will it take to have fewer than 1,000 bowls of ice cream left?

Side Dish (at least 1)

- Create a graph of the data for the rapid decay of ice cream in the world.

- What if it was decreasing at a massive 45% but only every 5 minutes? Now how long would it take to have fewer than 1,000 bowls?

Desserts (as many as you like)

- Find a graph in research that represents either a logarithmic function or an exponential function that deals with radioactive decay and explain its similarity to the ice cream situation.

- Create and explain your own problem with radioactive decay.

- Invent and create your own dessert that deals with radioactive decay (clear your plan with Mr. Sager).

SOURCE: Used with permission of Dale Sager.

cream—see Figure 5.6); he then built in several side-dish and dessert choices to serve as situational motivators.

When Mr. Sager began using Learning Menus, he found that students moved to menu work when they finished other class work; this helped him deal with the ragged finish time he often encountered in his flipped classroom due to the increased flexibility afforded by this model (for more about this, see Chapter 6). He allowed students to work on their menus at home or at school, and in collaborative or individual settings, depending on students' preferences. His expectation was that all students complete the assigned menu before the unit's end, and he often found that menu work served as a helpful tool for review.

Mr. Sager's menu was an informal tool for harnessing students' varying interests and learning profiles. Like RAFTs, Learning Menus can be designed with summative assessment in mind, calling on the teacher to build in more structure, description, and accountability. Examples of extended menus illustrating these principles of summative assessment can be found in Appendix C.3.

TriMind

The TriMind strategy presents students with a more specific kind of choice—that is, assignment options designed to appeal to the different ways students may prefer to process information. In broad terms, this strategy appeals to students' *learning profiles*. TriMind uses cognitive scientist Sternberg and Grigorenko's (2007) "Triarchic" Theory as a basis for constructing assignment options designed to appeal to analytical, practical, and creative thinkers. This approach focuses on expanding the kind of instructional options offered in the classroom with the goal of harnessing every student's strengths.

According to Sternberg, the human intellect comprises three sets of abilities:

1. **Analytical:** The ability to analyze, compare/contrast, see the parts and the whole, examine cause and effect, and think in linear and logical-sequential ways

2. **Practical:** The ability to put ideas into action, apply knowledge and skills to the real world, execute tasks efficiently, and problem-solve/resolve conflict on-the-spot

3. **Creative:** The ability to imagine possibilities, think outside the box, innovate, invent, ask insightful questions, propose novel solutions, or intuit

School typically emphasizes analytical intelligence, often at the expense of developing or valuing practical and creative intelligence. If teachers used a balance of analytical, practical, and creative tasks/assessments to convey information and monitor understanding, they might find that more students would successfully navigate and master required content (Sternberg & Grigorenko, 2007). Therefore, teachers should provide students with options for how they want to process material that are aligned to analytical, creative, and practical ways of thinking. See Figures 5.7 and 5.8 for specific examples of classroom applications.

As with the other three strategies discussed in this section, there are certain steps to follow to increase the quality of TriMind choices:

1. Begin by choosing the standard and aligned learning goals you want each option to address.

2. Generate three tasks—all aligned with the same learning goals—that appeal to creative, practical, and analytical thinkers.

3. When designing tasks, remember that the terms Analytical, Practical, and Creative refer to types of *thinking* rather than to particular kinds of *products*. For example, Creative tasks should emphasize innovative and fresh thinking rather than artistic responses. Analytical tasks should push students toward investigations and evaluations rather than toward creating charts or diagrams. Practical tasks should emphasize real-world use rather than the creation of simple checklists.

4. Present tasks as OPTIONS to students rather than diagnosing and assigning them. It's also best to avoid labeling the tasks; rather, present them as Option 1, 2, and 3. That way, students will select the tasks (rather than the labels) that most appeal to them. (*Note:* Task options in the figures are labeled for *teacher information*, not for students to see when they are making their choices.)

The TriMind examples in Figures 5.7 and 5.8 can be used as processing tools either at home or at school. The reading response choices could be offered as discussion board prompt choices or in-class journal responses. The social studies tasks could be assigned as homework to follow up on in-class document analysis or used as in-class processing choices for students to display what they learned from at-home examinations of current events in the media. In any case, they motivate students by providing choice, and provide teachers with a means of Flexible Grouping, because students can work in like-preference groups and share in mixed-preference groups. This holds true whether using TriMind for lesson-level checks (like Figures 5.7 and 5.8) or for more formal summative checks. If TriMind is to be used as a means of summative assessment, it is imperative that teachers include detailed task instructions and construct rubrics that are tightly aligned to the unit's learning goals (see Appendix C.4). More formal TriMind assignments like those displayed in the Appendix can be used as performance assessments that students work on throughout the course of the unit or as anchor activities for them to move to when they finish other work.

FIGURE 5.7: ELA READING RESPONSE OPTIONS

Standard:
CCSS.ELA-LITERACY.CCRA.R.3
Analyze how and why individuals, events, or ideas develop and interact over the course of a text.

Finish reading _____, then choose and complete one of the following:

Analytical	Practical	Creative
Analyze the behavior of each of the "major players" in this section and give a description of what each one is like. Include important details of what they say and do in your descriptions, and describe how others respond to them. You can display your findings in a chart or table, if you wish.	Your classmate was absent on the day the class read and discussed this selection. Write a note explaining the scene to him or her. Be sure to describe all the major players' statements and actions (and others' reactions TO them), and explain their importance/role. Make sure you do so in a language/manner that you know your friend will understand.	Imagine what it would be like to be _____ (celebrity, another character, etc.) who has secretly witnessed this scene or selection unfold. Rewrite the scene from this new perspective. Be sure to include the key conversations and actions of all major characters (importance/role), but put this new narrator's "spin" on it.

FIGURE 5.8: SOCIAL STUDIES HISTORICAL OR CURRENT EVENTS PROCESSING OPTIONS

Standard:

CCSS ELA-Literacy.RH.9–10.6

Compare the point of view of two or more authors for how they treat the same or similar topics, including which details they include and emphasize in their respective accounts.

Analytical	Practical	Creative
Read the two accounts of _____.	Read the two accounts of _____.	Read the two accounts of _____.
Present a point-by-point analysis of the details and ideas that differ between the two accounts. Then, write an analysis that explains (1) why you believe two differing accounts exist and (2) how credible you believe each of authors' perspectives to be and why.	Recommend to a friend the version of the account that *you* believe to be most accurate. Support your recommendation with explanations of (1) the differences between the two accounts and (2) the reason behind those differences (e.g., why one perspective is more believable than the other).	Take on the voice of one of the authors and write a critique or "rebuttal" of the other account. Be sure to discuss (1) the points where your accounts differ, (2) why you believe the other author got those points wrong, and (3) what the other author might study or consider to change his/her perspective.

USING THE STRATEGIES EFFECTIVELY

All four strategies outlined in this chapter can be utilized at the lesson level to monitor students' grasp of smaller chunks of learning goals. All four can also be used at the conclusion of a unit to gauge student understanding of a larger body of principles, content, and skills. In either case, the teacher must take care to craft assignment options keeping the following "criteria for success" in mind (Doubet & Hockett, 2015):

- All assignment options should address the same standards and learning goals.

- All assignment options should require the same degree of rigor (unless strategic readiness adjustments are made; such adjustments will be discussed within the context of each strategy).

- All assignment options should appear equally respectful to students.

- All assignment options should be accompanied by clear task descriptions and transparent expectations/criteria for success.

- Allow students to propose alternative options that the teacher can approve *if* those options adhere to each of the criteria listed above.

- Make sure assignment options offer a true variety of approaches rather than multiple versions of the same kind of thinking.

- All assignment options should be able to be assessed using the same rubric (this helps ensure alignment of learning outcomes and streamlines the evaluation process).

Additionally, given the unique dynamics of a flipped classroom, we also offer the following additional criteria:

- At-home assignment options should utilize technology to *facilitate* the engagement of student interest, not as a means *for* interest-based differentiation, in and of itself.

- At-home assignment options should be made clear to students *prior* to leaving class that day so that students are aware of their options and the associated expectations.

THE BOTTOM LINE

Used properly, the strategies for harnessing student interest discussed in this chapter provide teachers of flipped classrooms with tools for motivating students to demonstrate their grasp of important content while fostering task-investment, student collaboration, and Flexible Grouping. All strategies acknowledge and capitalize on the reality that "[w]e will seek out and pay attention to things we already know about in an effort to increase our knowledge base" (Hattie & Yates, 2014, p. 6). In addition, these strategies help shape the classroom, and the at-home learning environment, into places where students begin to see their differences as an asset—as something to be celebrated rather than to be ignored or avoided. As an eleventh grader explained, "It helps me to learn how to work with other people who have different kinds of skills, opinions—just really learn how to work with a multitude of people" (Doubet, 2007, p. 238).

A TEACHER IN ACTION

It was the beginning of a new school year, and Ms. Velazquez felt she was entering this semester armed with many tools for building community, assessing her students in informal and formal manners, and adjusting instruction to meet the varying readiness needs of her students. Her growth last year was profound, and she was incredibly satisfied with how much more effectively she was capitalizing on the flexibility offered by the Flipped model and as well as on the learning potential of her students!

Before she left for the summer, however, she had written down two areas in which she wanted to "shake things up" even more the following year: Flexible

Grouping and student investment. She had grown accustomed to using both random and readiness groupings, but even she grew weary of Fold the Line and Team Huddles when she used them day after day. She wondered if her students felt the same way. She also wondered how she could help her students better see that mathematics was connected to their everyday lives. She thought infusing those kinds of connections might add additional "flavor" to what had become her normal classroom fare.

Over the summer—as part of her professional-learning-community work—Ms. Velazquez did some reading on student motivation; she also attended a conference on instructional strategies designed to foster investment in learning. She felt that—by adding some of these new ideas into what she was already doing—she might increase students' interest both in mathematics and in each other as people.

She planned to begin the year collecting Student Interest Cards (see Figure 5.1) to help both her students and herself to begin thinking about potential connections between their pastimes and mathematics. She knew those cards would help her find ways to offer interest-based Practice Problems, Journal Prompts, and Four-Corners activities as well. By grouping students—both online and in class—according to those shared interests, she felt her grouping configurations would feel more fluid than they had the previous year . . . and she hoped students would naturally bond over shared interests.

But she needed to do some up-front planning for the more structured activities she wanted to employ. She planned to use a Learning Menu, RAFT, or TriMind assignment each quarter to provide students with work to move to when they had completed their regular class work. She would design these assignments so that they (1) offered choice in how students practiced and showcased their work, (2) provided new ways for students to work together to both construct and share responses, (3) presented options for more engaging review activities, and (4) asked students to produce learning in a more performance-based manner (a recent emphasis in her district). She vowed to space these strategies out to one per quarter to make sure both she and her students were ready for the change.

CHAPTER 6

Managing the Differentiated Flipped Classroom

Ms. Velazquez sat at her desk after school surveying her folders (electronic and manila) of "incoming work." They had changed significantly since her implementation of several new interest-based strategies this quarter. It wasn't an issue of *more* assignments; it was simply the added layer of dealing with *different* assignments. Students often completed different problems in class, responded to different discussion threads for homework, selected different RAFT strips for processing options, and so on. And in the case of this quarter's Learning Menu, she wasn't entirely sure *where* students were in their progress, since they worked on their menus at the completion of class work (which was at different times for different students).

She was energized by the increased investment she'd noticed in her students. They were more motivated to complete assignments, more on-task during class work, and had bonded in ways she had not anticipated. But students' increased comfort with one another had—in part—increased the noise level in class. It was "good" noise, she knew, but it was something else to deal with. The changes were worth it; of that she was *absolutely* certain, but she confessed to herself that she felt overwhelmed at times. She needed to employ systems for record keeping, dealing with noise and movement, and so on.

FLEXIBILITY REVISITED

We began this book by discussing flexibility as both a blessing and a curse. As Ms. Velazquez's experience demonstrates, differentiating the flipped classroom results in tremendous blessings regarding the ability to meet students' needs, motivate them, hold them accountable, and move them all forward in their learning regardless of where they begin. In doing so, however, we more obviously reveal the need for systems for record keeping, monitoring individual progress, providing guidelines for group and independent work, and so on. Granted, such needs are always present; it is simply easier to ignore them in less responsive classrooms.

But the successful management of responsive classrooms is a hallmark of the effective instructional environment. In fact, Hattie (2012) ranks classroom management in the top one third of influences on student achievement. Marzano, Marzano, & Pickering (2003) also discuss the strong effect classroom management has on student performance. These researchers discuss four specific factors in their conception of management, including (1) the collaborative establishment of rules and procedures; (2) the effective handling of disciplinary interventions; (3) the establishment of healthy teacher–student relationships (which

> The successful management of responsive classrooms is a hallmark of the effective instructional environment.

we discussed in Chapter 2); and (4) maintaining the proper "mental set"—proactivity, focus and "withitness."

In our work with teachers, we find that the establishment and maintenance of rules, policies, and procedures are those areas that cause teachers the most concern. These policies include

- Classroom routines (e.g., use of electronics)

- Expectations for group work (e.g., submitting work, early finishers)

- Logistical concerns (e.g., noise and movement)

- Record keeping/progress monitoring

Therefore, those are the issues we tackle head-on in this chapter, presenting strategies for addressing them both at home and at school in a proactive manner. It is essential that classroom expectations (rules, routines, and procedures) be made clear to students, but it is equally important that students have opportunities to experience and practice these expectations both initially and periodically throughout the year. Anyone attending a live sporting event will notice that athletes typically have very regimented pregame routines. These don't just happen because the coach says so; these pregame routines are introduced *and* practiced until the coach is confident that the team or athlete can complete these routines automatically. Further, it is likely that the coach might need to revisit these routines from time to time as the crispness of execution fades. The same could and should be expected of any classroom. Likewise, the routines and procedures we discuss must be clearly introduced at the beginning of the year, and then maintained through practice and review as the year progresses.

> Anyone attending a live sporting event will notice that athletes typically have very regimented pregame routines. These don't just happen because the coach says so; these pregame routines are introduced *and* practiced until the coach is confident that the team or athlete can complete these routines automatically.

CLASSROOM ROUTINES: AT SCHOOL

An effectively managed classroom is complex. Emmer, Evertson, and Worsham (2003) note the importance of a system of rules and procedures for a well-run classroom: "It is just not possible for a teacher to conduct instruction or for students to work productively if they have no guidelines for how to behave or when to move about the room, or if they frequently interrupt the teacher or one another" (p. 17).

Based on the literature on classroom management and the dynamics of a flipped class-room at school, we suggest that teachers focus particular attention on (1) beginning and ending class and (2) the use of materials and equipment. In addition to the ideas presented in this section, a table of at-home and at-school management "trouble spots" is included at the end of this chapter (Figure 6.8 on pages 93–96) to serve as a quick troubleshooting guide for many of the common management issues that arise when managing the classroom both at home and at school.

Starting and Ending Class

When teaching in a differentiated flipped classroom, effective use of beginning and ending class routines is essential. First, teachers need to determine what students took away from viewing and processing the direct instruction the night before (and which students may have not watched at all). Second, teachers should not consider the lesson "complete" before they have (1) conducted one final check for under-standing and (2) ensured that expectations are clear for at-home assigned viewing.

When determining student understanding from the night before, teachers might use discussion threads or blog posts responding to the direct instruction that was pro-vided as an entrance card at the beginning of the following class (see Chapter 3). The results of these assessments might necessitate an adjustment to the planned instruc-tion (see Chapter 4). In addition, teachers should have a plan in place should stu-dents have failed to view or process the direct instruction. Much like students who unsuccessfully complete their homework to adequately prepare for class, students in a flipped class who do not complete the at-home portion assigned might be asked to take time at the beginning of class to watch and process the direct instruction and then join the rest of the class as they work on more engaging activities.

At the end of class, teachers should check on student understanding to ensure learn-ers are prepared for the at-home learning the teacher has planned. In addition, teach-ers must be sure that students (1) have the resources needed to access the content (e.g., Do they need to download a file before leaving if Internet access is a problem?) and (2) are clear about expectations for the assigned viewing and processing so that they can successfully complete the assignment.

Use of Materials, Equipment, and Personal Devices

Distribution, collection, and use of materials include computers, tablets, smartphones, and other resources. For successful differentiated flipping, teachers should develop, with the help of students, procedures so that all equipment and materials are distrib-uted and collected in a timely fashion. In addition, it is important to consider proper use and care of equipment and materials. In many schools, there are likely already regulations in place for distribution, collection, and proper use of technology. How-ever, if these regulations do not exist, teachers should develop these expectations, post them in the room, practice them at the beginning of the school year and also periodically throughout the rest of the year as necessary. What follow are two sample classroom policies for the distribution, use, and collection of technology. One is more open-ended (Figure 6.1) and the other more specific (Figure 6.2).

FIGURE 6.1: OPEN-ENDED TECHNOLOGY POLICIES: T.E.C.H.I.E.S.

T Teacher Time: When I say "eyes on me," screens need to be turned off.

E Every school-owned device must be signed out before it can be used.

C Connect to school Wi-Fi before using any device.

H Handle devices gently at all times.

I In case of damage, report it to the teacher immediately.

E Educational use: Devices are for educational use only.

S Safe Surfing: Be careful not to share passwords or personal information with others over the Internet. If you receive harassing messages, inform the teacher immediately.

FIGURE 6.2: SPECIFIC TECHNOLOGY POLICIES

1. Distribution

   - Only take the machine that you are assigned. Pick it up from and put it away in the designated slot.
   - Sign out your machine before taking it to your desk. You are responsible for the device you have signed out.
   - Carry devices with two hands at all times.

2. Care of Equipment

   - Report any broken pieces or malfunctions.
   - Be gentle with machines. Do NOT pull off keys or other pieces.

3. Use of Equipment

   - Visit only approved sites related to lesson.
   - When I need your attention, I will say "eyeballs on me," which means you need to turn off screens, close laptops, and place tablets and smartphones facedown on the front corner of your desk.
   - Devices should never be in your laps.
   - Keep your passwords confidential.

4. Use of Your Own Devices

   - If you want to use your own device, you must use it for school purposes only.
   - Personal devices must always be connected to school Wi-Fi network.
   - Turn off e-mail and text alerts prior to using personal devices.
   - No videos or pictures should be taken without permission from the teacher.
   - Make sure your device is fully charged at the start of the day.
   - Devices should be off and put away when not being used in class.
   - Devices are brought at the discretion of students and parents. Neither the teacher nor the school is responsible if the device is lost or damaged (see school use policy for additional information).

An often-voiced concern among teachers and administrators involves the use of student devices at school. More and more, schools are embracing the use of student-owned electronic devices (such as smartphones or tablets) for educational purposes through Bring Your Own Devices (BYOD) policies. During more recent school visits, we have noticed a significant increase in schools that have mobile device wireless networks allocated specifically for appropriate BYOD use. However, it is not enough just to assume students are always adhering to rules of proper use. There should be established school or classroom policies and consequences that are made clear to students with regard to BYOD use. See Appendix B for a sample school policy and teacher technology survey to gauge the availability and use of such devices. Such policies should also note that violating the established regulations could lead to disciplinary action just as with any other school policy infraction. By making expectations clear to students and including consequences for failing to meet those expectations, schools can take steps to ensure more appropriate use of technology in a classroom and school setting.

EXPECTATIONS FOR INDIVIDUAL AND GROUP WORK: AT SCHOOL

In a differentiated flipped classroom, a reduction in teacher-centered activities at school will necessarily lead to more individual and group activities. As such, there are several important management issues to consider:

- Submitting work
- What to do with early finishers
- Expectations for teacher-led activities

Routines for submitting student work are necessary when different students are submitting different work, either individually or in groups. A traditional method for regulating this is maintaining class folders or bins. However, due to the nature of a differentiated flipped classroom, much work will likely be stored electronically. Teachers should identify a format they are comfortable with (many schools subscribe to learning management systems such as Blackboard or Canvas), and then ensure that students are comfortable with this method as well. If your school does not subscribe to a learning management system, there are some tools are included in Appendix A that can facilitate the submission of student work (e.g., Google Drive and Edmodo).

A second concern is what students should do if they finish an individual or group activity while others are still working. One solution is establishing *anchor activities*, a routine essential for managing any differentiated classroom. These are activities that students automatically transition to when they have finished the assigned work for the day. Anchor activities should be "presented with clear directions so that students know what to do, what the final product should be . . . and what to do with the work they generate" (Tomlinson & Imbeau, 2010, p. 127). As discussed earlier, some of these anchor activities might be electronic in nature. For example, teachers might have students maintain a separate blog as an anchor activity (i.e., "Anchor Blog"), where they respond to challenging or curiosity-building extension questions when they are finished early. In a high school math class, students might work on several weekly challenge problems. Or, in a world language class, students might be expected to select a certain custom of interest to them and investigate it in the target culture, comparing it to a similar U.S. custom. Access to technology opens up doors to additional anchor activity strategies to implement when students finish early and can increase the inquiry potential of the interest-building activities discussed in Chapter 5 (e.g., Learning Menus, RAFTs, TriMind), which all can be used as anchor activities.

Expectations for Teacher-Led Activities

Although at-school, teacher-led instruction may decrease in a differentiated flipped classroom, teachers will still need to elicit and encourage student participation and engagement. One method of accomplishing this is through questioning—specifically ensuring high expectations for student involvement while respecting the various needs of students. Questioning is one of the most powerful tools in a teacher's arsenal. To use questions effectively, teachers should adhere to the following five principles:

Principle 1: Plan in Advance (Dean, Hubbell, Pitler, & Stone, 2012): The questions we come up with on the fly are often low-level and limit student opportunities to process and grapple with material. It takes more time to come up with analytical questions that ask students to synthesize what they've learned, defend their thinking, or make unusual connections. Taking time before class to prepare "chewy" questions (e.g., Webb's Depth of Knowledge Level 3–4 questions in Chapter 4) will ensure that we not only *ask* these important questions but that we *teach* in such a way to invite such higher order processing.

Principle 2: Apply "Mild Pressure" (Marzano, 2007): A common trap is to call on students when they look as if they are not paying attention so as to bring them back to attention. This is not the purpose of questioning. We can use questioning to make sure students are attending, but we should do this by applying "mild pressure." In other words, "if students realize there is a moderate chance of being called on to answer a question, it will likely raise their level of attention" (pp. 102–103). Think/Pair/Share—discussed in Chapter 4—offers one way to involve all students in answering the question. Investment is raised if they perceive they will be called on during the "share" phase.

Where applying mild pressure is concerned, we suggest two strategies that we have seen teachers use—and have used ourselves. The first of these is "Sticks of Accountability." Although not as elaborate as its grandiose name might suggest, this strategy involves putting students' names on Popsicle sticks—or having them create and decorate the sticks themselves—and placing them in a container (a Captain America or Wonder Woman coffee mug would be appropriate!). Teachers then randomly pull students' Popsicle sticks during the share phase of Think/Pair/Share—or after any sort of cue has been given that a question is coming. Alternately, apps like "StickPick," "TeachersPick," and others facilitate this same strategy in an electronic format.

A second technique for applying mild pressure is ClassDojo, an app and website that let you input your class rosters and track student behaviors. Once you have set up your class, there is a random feature that will select a student to answer a question. This allows teachers to digitally track student engagement when called on. Of course, with either questioning technique, should you notice one student who "needs to be called on"—for instance, a typically nonconfident student who has the correct answer—we don't see any problem with "randomly" choosing his or her name!

Principle 3: Strive for the Best Answer Possible (Lemov, 2010): When students respond to a question and their answer is 85% correct, the temptation is to congratulate the student instead of allowing them to grapple to get the answer completely right. We may chime in and say something like, "Nice answer! But let me clarify a couple of things." Rather than robbing students of the chance to refine their answers, however, the teacher should set the standard at 100% correct:

> The likelihood is strong that students will stop striving when they hear the word *right* (or *yes* or some other proxy), so there's a real risk in naming as right that which is not truly and completely right. When you sign off and tell a student she is right, she must not be betrayed into thinking she can do something she cannot. (Lemov, 2010, p. 35)

In other words, rather than diving in with quick congratulations, we should ask follow-up questions to help students reach complete understanding.

Principle 4: "No Opt Out" (Lemov, 2010): This principle asserts that it is never acceptable for a student to say, "I don't know" to a question. If a student were to indicate that he or she didn't know the answer, a teacher might let him or her ask for help or call on another student. However, the teacher then goes back to the original student and asks him or her to provide the correct answer as described by another student. This raises the level of expectations for student participation.

Principle 5: Support the Process: If students constantly get incorrect answers or are extremely shy of speaking up, we don't suggest you throw them into the fire unprepared. Simply communicating with these students ahead of time can help ease them into the class discussion. For example, teachers might share the question with these students ahead of time, communicating with them: "Do you know the answer to this question? If so I'm going to call on you" or "I know you don't like to speak up, but I want to help you work on your fear, I'm going to ask some questions today, and I will call on you to answer the first one. It's short, I promise." Second, it is likely that a combination of two or more of these used in conjunction with other questioning strategies (students raising hands, Think/Pair/Shares, etc.) will be the most effective way to address teacher-led management.

Logistical Concerns

Moving furniture, moving bodies, managing time, managing noise levels ... all these logistical concerns rise to the surface when we increase the fluidity of instruction. It is vital that teachers address these nuts and bolts in a proactive fashion to ensure that they become part of the fabric of how the classroom functions. One such logistical issue concerns communicating where students should sit during group work. This is a particularly sticky issue if a class utilizes desks instead of tables and operates within a small space. First, it is important to provide students with visual cues to illustrate where they are transitioning. One simple strategy involves using the draw feature and a text box on a Word Document. Figure 6.3 illustrates how teachers might create and save a drawing of their class, and then project it on the screen when students are getting into groups. Students would be assigned a color for their group membership for the activity, and then go to that spot in the class. Although the colored locations in the room stay the same, the group assignments vary depending on the intentions of the group work. For example, a student who is assigned to the purple group based on readiness one day might be assigned to the blue table the next day if students are grouped based on interest.

Teachers using this technique need not change their classroom diagrams; rather, they need only retype students' names in the textbox when groupings change.

FIGURE 6.3: CLASSROOM MAP FOR GROUP TRANSITIONS

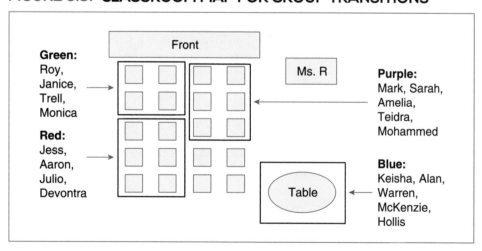

Alternatively, teachers can group students flexibly using the grouping feature on ClassDojo (app/website discussed earlier under Questioning Principle 2). This feature allows teachers to project student groupings to the screen or Smartboard. These groups of students can be randomized by the app or purposefully arranged by the teacher, and can easily be adjusted as needed.

In addition to knowing locations for group activities, it is important for students to move quickly in and out of their groups as well. To help with this expectation, teachers might put several different group configurations on the screen and have students practice getting into these groups. The principle of "practice makes permanent" holds up when building routines such as quick movement between groupings. We cannot expect students to get it unless they practice. An online timer (http://www.online-stopwatch.com/) can be projected so students are aware of the expected transition time. This same tool can also be used to show students how much time they have to work in these groups as well.

One of the most frequently cited management concerns is how to monitor and manage noise levels during group work. This is a valid concern, because too much noise can be an impediment to effective group work. The first hurdle may be for teachers to thoughtfully consider how much noise is acceptable, realizing that conversation is a must during collaboration. Once teachers determine their threshold for acceptable noise, they should make these expectations clear to students. One method teachers can use to model acceptable noise levels is playing music at a certain volume while students work in groups. If at any point the class noise level is above that of the music, students know they need to quiet down. Alternatively, teachers might download decibel meter applications (e.g., Decibel 10th, a free app and Decibel Meter Pro, a low-cost alternative) on their personal devices and practice different noise levels with students using these tools. Like the digital stopwatch, decibel meters can be used to both introduce and to monitor and/or communicate expectations regarding acceptable noise levels for academic conversations.

Although not an exhaustive list of effective classroom management categories and ideas, these components are essential to ensuring successful use of differentiation and flipping. Please refer to the "trouble spots" chart (Figure 6.8 on pages 93–96) for additional logistical management issues and solutions.

RECORD KEEPING: AT HOME AND AT SCHOOL

At Home: Record Keeping of Student Responses Through Discussion Posts, Blogs, or Journals

When students are participating in direct instruction at home, management primarily consists of keeping records of student responses to various active processing strategies. This raises two related issues: (1) How can teachers ensure that students come to school prepared with the necessary content to participate in class activities, and (2) What is an effective way to keep track of student completion and progress? We suggest a simple strategy adapted by Carbaugh (2014) from Fisher and Frey (2012) to **Keep Track of Student Completion and Readiness for Class** (see Figure 6.4). Teachers could briefly look over at-home student responses at the beginning of class, perhaps during a warm-up activity, and enter student data using their initials, assigning students a 0 (no effort), 1 (effort, but many errors present), or 2 (mostly correct with few errors present). An added benefit to a system like this is the ability to monitor student growth as well. If teachers keep track of multiple activities or formative assessments that address the same learning goals, then they should see a reduction in student errors in later assessments (if students are improving, errors should diminish). When working to develop persistence and a growth mindset in students, a system like this enables teachers to show students that their efforts are leading to growth toward specific standards or learning goals. This assessment system could be kept on a Google Drive spreadsheet, with access (but not editing) privileges provided to parents (see Appendix A for more information on Google Drive and Google Docs). Students could each be assigned a unique code so that parents could keep track of their child's at-home efforts and how these translate into class readiness.

The example in Figure 6.4, on the next page, utilizes the **Discussion Post** strategy outlined in Chapter 4, with two options for students differentiated based on readiness. Option 1 presents a greater challenge to students in the form of creating a mathematic scenario, while Option 2 still requires students to generate their own probability distribution, without the added elaboration. Next to each option are the initials of students who didn't attempt the problem (0), attempted it with significant errors (1), or those who correctly completed the problem, or completed it with few errors (2).

Finally, there is the very real need to teach, monitor, and hold students accountable for appropriate interactions, both at home and at school. It is no secret that people can take on different personas when communicating virtually versus face-to-face. Almost anyone who regularly communicates online has interacted with someone flexing his or her "Internet muscles," behaving in a way contrary to typical face-to-face means of communicating. Sadly, the rise of cyberbullying illustrates this notion all too clearly. In a differentiated flipped classroom, teachers should set clear expectations about student interactions and model appropriate online statements and responses. Such measures are part of establishing a community of learners as described in Chapter 2. However, teachers should be sure to clearly and regularly communicate with students about avoiding negative interactions in a virtual social setting. Further, should students fail to follow these guidelines, there should be a way for students to report these negative interactions to the teacher—anonymously, if necessary.

FIGURE 6.4: HIGH SCHOOL STATISTICS AND PROBABILITY COMPLETION AND READINESS LOG

Standard:

CCSS.MATH.CONTENT.HSS-MD.A.4

Develop a probability distribution for a random variable defined for a sample space in which probabilities are assigned empirically; find the expected value. For example, find a current data distribution on the number of TV sets per household in the United States, and calculate the number of sets per household. How many TV sets would you expect to find in 100 randomly selected households?

	Didn't Attempt (0)	Attempted With Significant Errors (1)	Completed the Problem With Few or No Errors (2)
Discussion Post Option 1 3-Minute Essay: Come up with a scenario where the following equation would help you solve for an expected value. Then create a probability distribution and solve for the expected value of X. $E(x) = x1p1 + x2p2 + \ldots + xipi.$	QP	WS, MM, JS, AW	DF, JM, ES, JC
Discussion Post Option 2 Generate your own probability distribution and solve for the expected value of X. $E(x) = x1p1 + x2p2 + \ldots + xipi.$	DS, KJ, AP	CC, LC, KD, JI	RJ, JT, FO

Tracking Progress: At Home and At School

Self-Assessment

Self-assessment is an important part of personalized learning and individual growth. To illustrate how this looks in the classroom and at home, let's revisit the Learning Menu strategy discussed in Chapter 5. When assigning Learning Menus, teachers must monitor student progress, including opportunities for students to self-assess the relationship between the effort they have invested and the progress they have made, with the hope that these are closely balanced. Little effort and great progress require intervention from the teacher, just as great effort and little progress do. Because teachers of flipped classrooms have created more flexible in-class experiences to facilitate more student-centered work, they should discover additional class time to confer with students who struggle to see the fruits of their effort, or who find little value added with the assignments they complete.

The **Self-Assessment** example pictured in Figure 6.5 illustrates how one student might rate his or her progress based on perceived effort on the Learning Menu used by Mr. Sager in Chapter 5 (Figure 5.6). If Mr. Sager were to view a self-assessment like this one, an intervention should follow since the student's hard work on the main courses is not leading to progress. Through scaffolding (as outlined in Chapter 4), he could help the student reap greater benefits from her effort invested. A simple self-assessment such as this one could be used for Learning Menus as well other strategies, whether completed at home or at school.

FIGURE 6.5: **STUDENT LEARNING MENU SELF-ASSESSMENT—PROGRESS AND EFFORT**

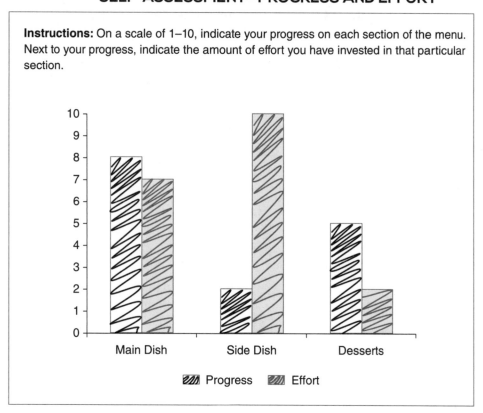

Instructions: On a scale of 1–10, indicate your progress on each section of the menu. Next to your progress, indicate the amount of effort you have invested in that particular section.

Student Persistence Logs

Persistent *teachers* strive to find something that works for every learner and seek to help students understand the role of mistakes in learning and growth. Persistent *students* identify key changes or corrections they must make to improve their learning outcomes. One way to achieve this in a differentiated flipped classroom is to have students maintain **Persistence Logs**. Students completing activities or products—both at school and at home—must understand that often the first attempt will not be their best work. Teachers looking to communicate this message to students could include opportunities to improve their thinking and quality of work. Returning to the Learning Menu example, students might rework sections of their menus after Mr. Sager's feedback. It is wise to have students indicate what they plan on improving before resubmitting particular portions of the menu. This way, students must think critically about where and how to focus their efforts. Figure 6.6 provides an example of what this might look like as Mr. Sager asks his students to become more persistent learners.

FIGURE 6.6: STUDENT LEARNING MENU PERSISTENCE LOG

	Main Course	Side Dish	Dessert
Teacher Feedback	Your work on the main dish is accurate, and you've illustrated and explained your thinking. Well done!	I see that you've tried both side dishes, but finished neither. For an illustration of the concept behind both, see last Wednesday's at-home video and your own response on the discussion post (which was on target!).	You tackled this strategically and succeeded. Have some more dessert! ☺
My Next Steps to Improve			

Reflective Prompts

To be effective classroom leaders, teachers must constantly reflect on their impact on student learning and ask students to reflect on what helps them be successful in the classroom. As illustrated with the Learning Menu example, teacher feedback on student work is one way to determine this, but another is to have students reflect on what worked for them, and what might help them improve next time. Consider a student's response to her work (Figure 6.7) on the TriMind Current Event Analysis assignment outlined in Chapter 5 (Figure 5.8). Since this particular assignment could be used repeatedly to analyze different historical and current events, student reflection is particularly important.

You have likely noticed that the practices of self-reflection, persistence, and reflection are very much interdependent. For example, persistence would be impossible were it not for reflection on what is needed to persist. It makes logical sense, then, to put these

FIGURE 6.7: STUDENT TRIMIND SELF-REFLECTION PROMPTS

Things that worked well for me were . . .	I did the prompt where I took on the voice of one author to criticize the work of the other author/perspective. I think I did a good job of arguing convincingly in his voice, but I only pointed out one difference in the two accounts. Now I see there were more. I just got so focused on the one that I didn't see the others.
Things that might be better for me in the future are . . .	I liked taking on the voice of the author and being able to be snarky like the author was—that part was fun—so I want to try that option again. But I should probably start by making a list of the differences that I want to address instead of just starting off by writing.

strategies together to better lead a differentiated flipped classroom. Appendix D shows how a teacher might use all these tools for a lesson on the Origins of the Civil War. It is vital that teachers lead their classroom such that students will consistently see themselves as a valuable, invited member of the class, where expectations remain high regardless of student needs. Teachers should strive to create an environment where each student is expected to persist, reflect, and invest in his or her learning.

TROUBLE SPOTS

We have addressed some strategies in depth, but we are well aware that many more exist. To help tie the elements of classroom environment together, Figure 6.8 provides typical trouble spots along with possible solutions that can aid teachers in leading and managing a flipped, differentiated classroom. Instructional strategies from earlier in the book are referenced when possible.

FIGURE 6.8: MANAGEMENT TROUBLE SPOTS

Trouble Spot	Possible Solutions
Participation	• Use the **Sticks of Accountability** or **ClassDojo** system to remind students that everyone is "fair game" to answer a question following think and/or pair time. • Utilize **Playing Cards** as a means for calling on students. Distribute cards—one per student—and use a second deck (real or electronic) to draw cards (that correspond to students' cards) as a means of random accountability.

(Continued)

FIGURE 6.8: (Continued)

Trouble Spot	Possible Solutions
Participation (continued)	• Utilize **Dice** the way you might use playing cards. Assign each group a number and each person in the group a number. Then roll two dice. The number on one die represents the *table number,* and the number on the other die represents the *student number.* If a four and a five were rolled, for instance, student four at table five must respond to the question.
Transitions	• Recognize that transitions must become part of the classroom **routine** and thus require **practice**. • Begin with **dry runs** of group movement, displaying groupings on the board and asking students to move to those grouping or stations in as little time and with as little noise as possible. • If you have more than one section of a class, record each class's time during dry runs and utilize **between-class competitions** to encourage efficiency of movement. • If—after a while—students begin to lag in their movements, institute a **review** and practice/race of dry runs to reinforce the need for efficiency. • Display a **Digital Stop Watch** and give **clear time limits** for all transitions between tasks and grouping configurations.
Controlling Noise	• **Play music** quietly in background; students must always be able to hear the music. • Project **decibel monitor** on screen and ask students to not exceed a certain level. • Establish varying **noise level expectations** for different kinds of work and color-code those expectations to cards displayed for different tasks (red, green, yellow, etc.).
Grouping	• Post **visual cues** and charts at the front of the room that students can consult to see where and with whom they will be working. • Use **Playing Cards** to place students in groups. Upon entry into the classroom, each student is given a playing card. They are then instructed to get into suit groups, number groups, color groups, or all three at different points in the class to encourage flexible grouping. Cards may be distributed randomly or purposefully (e.g., all students needing extra help are given a particular suit). • Use **Fold the Line**, **Four Corners**, or any of the other grouping strategies discussed in Chapter 2 to create groups quickly. • **Vary grouping configurations** as much as possible. Students should work individually, in pairs, and in small groups. Pairs/groups should be formed at random, by student choice, and by teacher analysis of interest or readiness.

Trouble Spot	Possible Solutions
Expectations for Group and Individual Work	• Post an **agenda/schedule** for the class. • Avoid giving multiple sets of instruction to the entire class; rather, present different groups with different task directions on **different task cards** (hard copy, electronically, or recorded). • Task cards should contain **detailed task instructions** so that students know exactly what is expected of them. • Provide students with access to different web resources using **QR codes**, which students can scan to efficiently arrive at their assigned site or appropriate online resources. QR Code Generators (e.g., http://www.qrstuff.com) can facilitate this. • Establish **checklists for quality work** so that students can both self-assess and peer-assess their progress. • Create **anchor activities** for students to move to when they complete a group task or individual work before time is called. Such activities should be engaging and be accompanied by clear instructions and criteria for success. • Describe what **"on task" behavior** looks like (via a checklist or rubric) and post this description in the class. Establish consequences for groups that are consistently off-task (e.g., disbanding the group). • Establish several **signals for getting the attention of the full class** to provide additional information or clarification, signal a transition, or draw attention to unsuitable noise. • Establish systems for students to use to garner assistance when working in groups (see **Cries for Help**—Chapter 3).
Use of Materials and Equipment (See Figures 6.1–6.2)	• As with all other policies and procedures, recognize that obtaining, using, and returning materials and equipment must become part of the classroom **routine** and thus require **practice**. • Establish a clear and comprehensive **protocol and policy** for the proper use—and for what constitutes misuse—of school equipment and personal electronic devices (see Appendix B for an example). • Create and post **"Helpful Hints" Resources** for students to use to troubleshoot common problems (e.g., "If your screen freezes . . .", "If you're having trouble printing . . .", "If your post does not appear . . ."). Make sure these troubleshooting guides are accessible both at home and at school.
Students Don't Do Homework	• Regard homework as **preparation** for in-class work and actively incorporate its results into beginning of class activities. • Regard homework as a **"ticket" to participating** in the group activities used to actively process it. Those students who do not have their homework should be allowed to sit in a **designated area of the room** to complete the homework and join in the discussion once it is completed.

(Continued)

Trouble Spot	Possible Solutions

Students Don't Do Homework (continued)	• Ensure that you are assigning homework in a **defensible manner**:
	
	  ○ Assessment and grading experts (e.g., O'Connor, 2011; Stiggins & Chappuis, 2005) generally agree that homework should **not be graded**; rather, it should be regarded as participation, checked for completion, and used as a teaching tool.
	
	  ○ Limit homework to a reasonable amount of **time** per evening. Prevailing recommendations (e.g., Cooper, Robinson, Patall, 2006) are for 10 to 20 minutes TOTAL per night in the first grade, and an additional 10 minutes per grade level thereafter (e.g., 50 minutes total for fifth grade, 100 minutes total for tenth). Note that these recommendations refer to total amount of time spent on homework rather than to homework per class. In other words, moving to flipped homework should not involve assigning more homework than should be assigned in a traditional classroom.

Students Disrespecting Each Other During Online Interactions	• Establishing **clear expectations for respect** online as a nonnegotiable part of creating a community of learners. • Clearly **discuss and model** how to avoid negative interactions in a virtual social setting. • **Monitor** student-student communications for red flags regarding comments, tone, and other such issues. • Establish a system for students to **report negative interactions**—anonymously if necessary. • Establish clear consequences for those who violate the principles of positive online interactions.

THE BOTTOM LINE

By its very nature, a flipped classroom brings with it a new set of management issues. This chapter has addressed many of these issues and provided a road map for a more effective learning environment, both at home and at school. Used in conjunction with classroom community and mindset discussed in Chapter 2, effective management provides the systems necessary to help students—and groups of students—function more autonomously and helps teachers spend more time tailoring their interactions with students. In other words, effective management provides the setting for the differentiated flipped classroom to capitalize on the blessing of flexibility.

Closing Thoughts

We opened this book by sharing a research study in which some viewers failed to notice strange events (e.g., gorillas, umbrellas) occurring in the background of videos they were studying (Chabris & Simons, 1999). This brief portrait of the issue of attention—or nonattention—launched our investigation of how to better ensure that students focus on and make sense of instruction in a flipped environment—both at home and at school.

The take-way message is that up-front, purposeful instructional decisions are necessary to ensure that student learning is maximized. Teachers cannot assume that the mere presence of technology or the ability to pause videos wields enough pedagogical value to assure that students are actively processing teacher-created or assigned at-home direct instruction. Further, teachers cannot assume that as a result of at-home learning experiences students are adequately prepared for in-class activities. Instead, teachers should proactively seek to find what works for students, and then to identify opportunities within a lesson to purposefully adjust for challenge and relevance based on assessment evidence.

Below are the key ideas discussed throughout the chapters of this book. Adhering to these can help safeguard against the gorilla in the background—or the food stuck in your teeth when you recorded your video—distracting from an otherwise effective learning experience.

SUMMARIZING THE OVERARCHING PRINCIPLES

The following eight key ideas present an overarching, interdependent framework for teachers seeking to leverage the added flexibility of a flipped classroom to meet the diverse needs of their students.

1. Both at-home and at-school learning experiences can be proactively differentiated based on student readiness, interest, and learning profile.

2. Cultivating student-student and student-teacher relationships and fostering a growth mindset are essential to creating a community of learners who feel in control of their success.

3. Ongoing formative assessment, both at home and at school, provides teachers with evidence of student learning to inform instructional decision making and to provide feedback to learners.

4. Attention to student readiness assists in moving all students forward by meeting students at appropriate cognitive levels.

5. By harnessing student interests and learning profiles, teachers strive to motivate students through relevance, choice, and preference.

6. At-home learning experiences should "prime" students for in-class activities by

- promoting active processing based on clearly identified learning goals and

- encouraging social interaction when possible and beneficial.

7. At-school learning activities should provide students with opportunities to wrestle with content in the company of peers for support and challenge.

8. Effective management, both at home and at school, provides the "systems" necessary to help students—and groups of students—function more autonomously and to help teachers spend more time tailoring their interactions with learners.

A TEACHER AT WORK

Ms. Velazquez's journey toward a differentiated flipped classroom enacted these key principles in the following ways:

Community

Recognizing that she could not make learning relevant or appropriately challenging for students she did not know, Ms. Velazquez began by taking active steps to build community (Chapter 2). She used **Attendance Questions** both at home and in school and regularly employed **Fold the Line** to create both random and purposeful in-class groupings. She fostered the growth mindset by asking students to view and create **Famous Failure** videos. In addition, she made sure that both her words and her actions sent "growth" messages by celebrating mistakes as stepping-stones to success and making sure students worked with classmates whom they would *challenge* as well as with classmates by whom they would *be challenged*.

Formative Assessment

She also began proactively checking in to see how her students were processing and making sense of information by employing varying means of accountability measures and formative assessment (Chapter 3). She combined **Self-Assessment** (e.g., rating understanding of at-home viewing) with more concrete modes of at-home interaction and processing checks by using **graphic organizers, discussion board** prompts, **backchannel chats** and **Padlet** boards. She also used **Padlet** check-ins at school, along with other formative assessment strategies such as **My Favorite No** and **Graffiti**. Such measures ensured there were no surprises when it came to students grasping—or failing to grasp—her lesson goals.

Adjusting for Readiness

Once Ms. Velazquez had a sense of what students needed, readiness wise, she adjusted her instruction to meet those varying learning needs (Chapter 4). She began by pulling small **Team Huddles** to address patterns discovered via formative assessment. When she became comfortable with that method—and aware of the fact that it wasn't always enough—she proactively designed targeted **small group tasks** using varying levels of **scaffolding** and **questioning**—both at home and at school—to provide every student with what they needed to grow.

Motivating Through Interest and Learning Profile Options

To harness motivation (Chapter 5), Ms. Velazquez offered her students processing options—both at home and at school—designed to target their interests and learning preferences. Through both low-prep strategies (e.g., **Interest-Based Prompts** to process at-home viewing) and more developed assignments (e.g., **TriMind assignments** to serve as summative learning checks), Ms. Velazquez learned more about her students as she saw them get excited about their chosen learning options and take their work in directions she had not previously imagined.

Grouping Flexibly

Not only did these interest-based measures increase student investment, but they also allowed Ms. Velazquez to group students with shared interests and preferences together, "shaking up" her grouping configurations beyond the readiness and random groups that she had been relying on. This increased use of **Flexible Grouping** (Chapters 2, 5, and 6) both strengthened classroom community—as students bonded over similarities—and ensured that no student felt "pigeonholed" into readiness groups.

Leading and Managing

As Ms. Velazquez became more flexible with her instruction, she discovered the need for more appropriate **management systems** (Chapter 6). To make sure her instructional plans flowed regarding logistics, she employed the following techniques:

- She established clear-cut **policies** for using technology in class (see Figure 6.2, page 83).
- To monitor group work and progress, Ms. Velazquez employed a **Colored Cups** system (Chapter 3, page 34) and **Process-Monitoring Logs** (Figure 6.4, page 90).
- To facilitate smooth transitions and reasonable noise levels, Ms. Velazquez posted **Classroom-Grouping Charts** to illustrate where students were to sit (Figure 6.3, page 87), enforced **time limits** during group transitions, and displayed her phone's **Decibel Meter** app on her document camera.
- To help students and/or groups of students access different videos, websites, and tutorials, Ms. Velazquez regularly distributed **QR Codes** (see

Figure 6.8, page 95); this ensured that everyone logged on to the correct site without logistical bumps and without drawing attention to differences.

- Because individuals and groups finished work at ragged times, Ms. Velazquez implemented **Learning Menus** and **RAFT** tasks for use as Anchor Activities. Each week students were responsible for completing a **Self-Assessment** of their progress (see Figure 6.7, page 93), which increased their sense of investment and accountability—and enabled Ms. Velazquez to maintain a sense of which students were completing which options.

With these management strategies in place, Ms. Velazquez truly felt as though she were capitalizing on every moment of her classroom time with students, and she felt more aware of and able to address questions that arose both *at home* and *at school*.

ENSURING PROGRESS

Two noteworthy patterns emerge from Ms. Velazquez's journey. First, she held a **growth mindset** (Dweck, 2006) for herself. Rather than feeling as if she had "arrived" after flipping her classroom, Ms. Velazquez sought out ways to make that structure work better for both her and her students. Furthermore, when things didn't go perfectly the first time she tried something (and they rarely did!), she pushed herself to fix what didn't work while holding on to what did. Rather than throwing the proverbial baby out with the bathwater, she maintained the aspects of strategies that worked and adjusted those that didn't to ensure a better fit for both her and her students.

> We must allow ourselves time to implement, practice, adjust, and settle into new routines if we are to be "in it for the long haul."

Second—and vitally important—Ms. Velazquez **did not make all her changes at once**. The journey on which we have followed her took more than 2 years . . . and it could have taken much longer! As she experimented with techniques for differentiating her flipped classroom, she started small, using the successful implementation of a few strategies to propel her into piloting a few more strategies. This "additive" effect gave both teacher and students time to get used to changing structures, to practice routines, and to adjust to new expectations. It is often tempting for teachers to try to do or to change everything at once. We must allow ourselves time to implement, practice, adjust, and settle into new routines if we are to be "in it for the long haul."

WHAT DOES IT LOOK LIKE IN "REAL TIME"?

Because Ms. Velazquez's journey represents change over time, we have included several snapshots of what a day or two of differentiated, flipped instruction might look like in various content areas. Appendix E contains four lesson plans (language arts, math, science, and social studies) that illustrate the ebb and flow between at-home and at-school learning and how to employ the strategies discussed in this book in both settings. Also included is a Flipped Lesson Plan (FLP) template, which can serve as a resource for teachers seeking to plan differentiated flipped instruction. The strategies featured in each FLP are summarized in Figure 7.1.

It is our hope that these lesson plans and the associated template—along with all the other resources presented in this book—will provide teachers with the support necessary to craft the active, responsive instructional experiences our students need and deserve.

FIGURE 7.1: STRATEGIES FEATURED IN EACH FLP

FLP Content Area	Strategies Featured
ELA	At Home: • Discussion Board for interest-based posts • Graphic Organizer for active processing • Padlet.com for formative assessment At School: • Padlet.com for modeling • Google Survey for formative assessment • Varying task complexity for Readiness Differentiation • Exit Slips for formative assessment Both Settings: • TriMind assignment for summative assessment
Math	At Home: • YouTube (socratica) for content viewing • Graphic Organizer for processing (adjusted for Readiness) • www.livejournal.com blogs for student posting and interaction At School: • Readiness Differentiation (additional Scaffolding) • Graphic Organizer for formative assessment Both Settings: • Learning Menu for summative assessment

FLP Content Area	Strategies Featured
Science	At Home: • www.todaysmeet.com for student interaction • TEDEd video for content viewing • www.kidblog.com for processing • Readiness Prompts based on Webb's DOK Framework At School: • Mixed Readiness Groups to facilitate Flexible Grouping • Graphic Organizer for active processing • RAFT for processing options based on student interest • Exit Slip for formative assessment
Social Studies	At Home: • Discussion Board for video processing • Padlet.com for formative assessment • www.kidblog.com for formative assessment and online student interaction At School: • Padlet.com for modeling • Think/Pair/Share for student interactions • Class Dojo for formative assessment • Four Corners for Flexible Grouping • Jigsaw for interest-based inquiry and Flexible Grouping • Google Docs for active processing and sharing in Jigsaw

START SMALL . . . BUT START

The path to transforming instruction does not start with huge leaps, but rather with small, next steps. The key to success is identifying the strategies that seem to make the most sense for you—in your setting—and launching from there. Begin by identifying the areas of your instruction that are in greatest need of becoming more proactive and responsive; then, choose and experiment with the tools in this book that address those issues. Once you and your students become familiar with those first steps, experiment with a few more. Where or *how* you begin your path toward a differentiated flipped classroom is not as important as simply *taking that first step*—no matter what that step is—to move forward on your own personal journey. We hope this book helps illuminate your path.

> The path to transforming instruction does not start with huge leaps, but rather with small, next steps.

APPENDIX A

Resources for Implementing a Flipped Classroom

In this appendix, we list some potential technology resources to help make a differentiated flipped classroom a reality. It is important to note, however, that by the time this book is published and read, some of the tools may have been improved on or replaced altogether. As such, we also provide you with some websites that are frequently updated to reflect new information that is available. Regardless of the tools used, the principles for differentiating a flipped classroom remain the same. The focus should be less on *what* tools are used, but rather on *how* these tools are used to improve student learning.

Also included in the descriptions of resources are links to tutorials with information on using them. Since many of the tools available have similar capabilities, we suggest teachers narrow their focus by considering the purpose of the tools before exploring the many options. This will help prevent the use of tools that are a poor fit for the desired outcome. For example, if an English teacher believes that screencasting tools are most appropriate for recording brief PowerPoint presentations, then it would be best to focus his or her efforts there. However, if a math teacher is intimidated by the notion of creating videos, then he or she should concentrate on sites like TeacherTube and Khan Academy, or a content personalization tool like eduCanon. The bottom line is, because of the sheer number of tools available, simply diving in without a clear purpose is at best confusing and at worst dissuading. Figure A.1 lists these resources within their respective categories. Brief descriptions and tutorial links are provided after the figure.

FIGURE A.1: FLIPPED RESOURCES BY CATEGORY

Category	Resources
General Information and Resources on Flipping *These sites provide updated information on resources for those looking to flip their classrooms.*	• Edudemic.com/guides/flipped-classrooms-guide/ • Flippedclass.com • Flippedlearning.org • Washington.edu/teaching/teaching-resources/engaging-students-in-learning/flipping-the-classroom/
Ready-Made Videos and Direct Instruction *Here teachers can find premade video links that can be sent to students to watch.*	• iTunes U (part of iTunes store) • Khanacademy.org • Knowmia.com • Learnzillion.com • Teachertube.com • Udemy.com • Youtube.com/education • Youtube.com/user/crashcourse
Video and Screencast Creation Tools: Computer Based *These tools can be used to create and record presentations in several different formats on or through a PC or Mac.*	• Adobe Captivate (software) • Camtasia (TechSmith product) • Computer Camera Recording • Document Camera Recording • Relay (TechSmith product) • Screencast-O-Matic.com • Screencastify.com (Google product) • SnagIt (TechSmith product) • Sophia.org
Video and Screencast Creation Tools: App/Tablet Based *These tools can be used to create and record presentations in several different formats on or through a tablet or smartphone.*	• Educreations • Explain Everything • Knowmia • Periscope • ShowMe • Tablet or Smartphone Recording • Verso

(Continued)

Category	Resources
Resources to Upload and Store Video Files *These sites can be used to house teacher- or student-created videos or screencasts.*	• Edmodo.com • TeacherTube.com • Weebly.com • Wikis • YouTube.com
Content Personalization Tools *These sites let users take existing videos and add questions, sound, and so on to adapt them to your learning goals.*	• eduCanon.com • EDpuzzle.com • Ed.Ted.com (TED Ed) • Zaption.com
Formative Assessment Tools *These apps and sites provide tools for checking on student understanding both at home and at school (see Chapter 3 for more information).*	• Evernote • Google Apps (Docs, Forms, and Hangout) • Getkahoot.com (Kahoot) • Padlet.com • Plickers.com • Polleverywhere.com • Socrative.com
Backchannels *These sites can be used to facilitate real-time conversation during at-school group work or at-home direct instruction viewing.*	• Backchannelchat • Chatterous.com • Chatzy.com • Google Hangout • Todaysmeet.com • Twitter.com
Blogs *These resources can be used for students to record thoughts and responses to assigned processing questions and activities.*	• Blogger.com • Blogster.com • Kidblog.org • LiveJournal.com
Varied Levels of Texts *These resources provide varied levels of readings on the same topic, current events, etc.*	• Booksthatgrow.com • Commonlit.org • Newsela.com • Readworks.org

GENERAL RESOURCES ON FLIPPING

www.edudemic.com/guides/flipped-classrooms-guide: This is a teacher's guide to classroom flipping, including key resources and articles on flipping.

Flippedlearning.org: This site houses tutorials, sample videos, research, and other resources to help teachers flip their classroom.

Flippedclass.com: This site has a great deal of information on flipping your classroom, including technology tools to get you started flipping.

www.washington.edu/teaching/teaching-resources/engaging-students-in-learning/flipping-the-classroom: Housed by the University of Washington's Center for Teaching and Learning, this site contains quick guides and start-up kits, videos, blogs, and various articles to support teachers looking to flip their classrooms.

READY-MADE VIDEOS

As we've mentioned throughout this book, teachers wishing to flip their class need not reinvent the wheel each time at-home content is needed. Teachers can choose from numerous videos from a variety of sources (e.g., www.khanacademy.org, www.knowmia.com, www.youtube.com/education, learnzillion.com, teachertube.com, and iTunes U). However, we caution that, should you choose to use videos that were made by other educators or organizations, you view them first in their entirety to determine alignment with your standards or learning goals. Showing students a video or other direct instructional tool that lacks alignment with the learning outcomes would be akin to assigning a problem set on inequalities during a unit on graphing equations. We suggest that teachers who wish to start by using existing videos also consider modifying them, using some of the content personalization tools listed below.

VIDEO AND SCREENCAST CREATION TOOLS (COMPUTER-BASED)

Techsmith Camtasia: This resource can be used to create and share professional videos, either through computer recording or importing videos from cameras, cell phones, or other recording devices. There is an app that easily transfers videos from mobile devices to Camtasia for editing. Users must purchase this software. A selection of video tutorials can be found here: http://www.techsmith.com/tutorial-camtasia-8.html

Screencast-O-Matic: This free software (basic version) allows users to record and publish videos and screencasts. There is a Pro version that has more capabilities but must be purchased (currently $15 per year). Here is a tutorial: https://www.youtube .com/watch?v=jADJ_OoSnm8

SnagIt: This product facilitates screen capturing and content recording. The user can save the presentation as a MP4 and then distribute the link to students. A tutorial can be found here: http://www.techsmith.com/education-video-how-to-lesson-mac.html

Adobe Captivate (http://www.adobe.com/products/captivate.html): This software, once installed, allows users to upload and then record sound over PowerPoint presentations as well as screenshots. Newer versions of the software have increased capabilities. Here is an introduction: https://www.youtube.com/watch?v=laC6Brkfmy4

Techsmith Relay: This tool allows users to create videos or screen captures. In addition, teachers can add questions to presentations and then view in-depth analytics of student responses. An overview of this resource and a variety of tutorial videos can be found here: http://www.techsmith.com/tutorial-techsmith-relay.html

Screencastify: This is a screencasting and video recording tool that can be used directly with the Google Chrome Internet browser. Once downloaded, the content of the user's browser, webcam, or desktop can be recorded. Videos can then be uploaded and shared through YouTube or Google Drive. A tutorial can be found here: https://www.youtube.com/watch?v=eC5AzFH5QfA

Sophia: This tool allows teachers to find or create tutorials about a range of topics. Many of the premade tutorials are aligned with Common Core and Next Generation Science Standards. Tutorials can be grouped together in "playlists" based on a topic, and then grouped again as a "pathway," which is essentially a unit-level grouping. Teachers can also become "Flipped Classroom Certified" by completing a free Sophia certification program. A tutorial for Sophia can be found here: https://www .youtube.com/watch?v=lX-BGS79u9g

Computer and Document Camera Recording: More than likely, any computer, smartphone, or tablet device has the capability to record videos (or if not, a webcam can be purchased inexpensively). Teachers can record themselves solving problems at a chalkboard, going through a history lecture on a brief PowerPoint, or demonstrating the organization of the periodic table of elements, and then upload the video to one of the sites discussed in the next section (youtube.com, edmodo.com, teachertube.com, etc.). Additionally, teachers who have document cameras can connect these directly to their computers and then record what is happening on their screen, just as they would a presentation. So, for example, a teacher wishing to show students the steps involved in solving a math problem could work these out under the document camera while their screencasting software captures the step-by-step method of solving the problem on their computers, which can then be uploaded for students to watch.

VIDEO AND SCREENCAST CREATION
TOOLS CONTENT CREATION (TABLET-BASED)

Explain Everything: This Android and Apple screencasting app is available for purchase at a relatively low cost and allows users to create and import content on their screen and then record sound to go along with the images and content on the screen. This app also has the ability to export content to YouTube or Dropbox for students to access. Tutorials for this app are available for free on youtube.com: https://www.youtube.com/watch?v=b00ZeszvjP4

Knowmia: This tablet-based content creation tool application allows teachers to construct presentations and embed videos within them. Included in the app is a tutorial that takes users through the content creation process. Here's a tutorial: https://www.youtube.com/watch?v=vB45lzKRTDA

Educreations: This is a screencasting tool for iPad that lets users animate and narrate selected content and post the products. Here is a tutorial: https://www.youtube.com/watch?v=oer20QtZdMo

Verso: This app lets teachers share videos they have found on the Internet with their students, along with discussion questions called "challenges." Students must download the app to access the content, but once they do, teachers can monitor student activity. A brief tutorial can be found here: http://versoapp.com/getting-started/

ShowMe: Exclusively for the iPad, ShowMe is a whiteboard app that allows the user to record voice-overs while writing on the virtual whiteboard. Images can also be dropped onto the whiteboard to be included in the presentation. Recordings can be uploaded directly to ShowMe and can be made public or kept private. Teachers can also search existing recordings to provide to students. A tutorial can be found here: https://www.youtube.com/watch?v=dUKv1S9Qoos

Periscope: A live video streaming app for Apple and Android devices, this tool allows you to broadcast material to a public or invited audience. Content can be viewed live or played back up to 24 hours later; videos can also be saved to the broadcaster's phone. Teachers can use this tool to broadcast to other classrooms (in the building or anywhere in the world), to project a remote audience into their own classrooms, or to stream brief tutorials to students working on homework. Viewers can post comments or questions during the broadcast, which also makes Periscope a potential formative assessment tool. To see other potential uses, visit www.periscope.tv

Tablet or Smartphone Recording: More than likely, any of these devices have the capability to record videos. As with computer or document camera, teachers could record lessons, perhaps solving problems at the chalkboard or going through a history lecture on a brief PowerPoint, and then upload them to one of the sites discussed in the next section (youtube.com, edmodo.com, etc.).

RESOURCES FOR UPLOADING AND STORING VIDEOS

Many of the above resources have the capability to store created content. However, it may be that teachers prefer recording videos and uploading them to class websites, learning management systems, and so on. Below are some easy-to-use resources for uploading and storing videos.

YouTube: This is the most commonly referenced place to upload videos. Users can create a "channel" for their class and upload and store videos so that students can revisit content. Teachers can also adjust the privacy settings so that only individuals who have the links can access the videos. For a tutorial on how to upload videos to YouTube: https://www.youtube.com/watch?v=Hlxqk0iHp5w

Edmodo: This is a free learning-management system that teachers can use to post videos to their class, as well as to add discussion threads, quizzes, assignments, polls and other resources for students to access. For a set of tutorials visit https://support .edmodo.com/home#entries/25546009-video-tutorials

Wikis: Wikis are essentially spaces where users can add, store, and modify content. There are a variety of wikis available for educators (Googlesites, Wikispaces, PB Works, etc.), and most have similar features, such as posting videos, files, discussions, and so on, but with the added benefit that students can collaborate with one another on common documents. For example, after watching an at-home video on quality online sources for history research, students might be asked to research and post links of sources they deem effective to the class wiki. Tutorials can be found online for the various wikis (e.g., here is a tutorial for PB Works: http://www.teacher trainingvideos.com/blogs-wikis-pb-works.html).

Weebly: This is a free and easy-to-use website creation source. Teachers could create class websites and post videos for students to access. For a list of tutorials, visit http:// hc.weebly.com/hc/en-us/sections/200354313-Beginner-s-Guide-to-Weebly

Teachertube: In addition to viewing videos that other teachers have uploaded, users can upload their own videos here as well once they sign up for a free account.

CONTENT PERSONALIZATION TOOLS

These resources allow teachers to pull from existing content and personalize it for their classes, including embedding questions and adding text.

eduCanon: This is a free website that allows users to upload content videos, crop them to desired length, and add strategically planned questions directly into the videos that can be used for active processing and/or as formative assessments to check for understanding. The finished videos are called "bulbs." Teachers can also add class rosters so that students can access content. A tutorial can be found at http://www.educanon.com/tutorial; and there is an entire YouTube channel dedicated to helping users with this tool: https://www.youtube.com/user/eduCanon

EDpuzzle: This is a free resource where users can upload a video to the site and then crop the video, record their voice over the video, embed a formative assessment, and then store the newly created content to the EDpuzzle site. A tutorial is provided once users sign up. An outside tutorial can also be found here: https://www.youtube.com/watch?v=dGK5qAe4Dck

TED Ed: This site has premade videos that can be personalized by adding thinking and discussion questions, context and other resources to support the video, and concluding thoughts when the video is over. Teachers can publish their videos and provide students with the link. A detailed set of tutorial videos for teachers wishing to use this tool can be found here: http://www.teachertrainingvideos.com/video-youtube/ted-ed.html

Zaption: This tool also lets users modify their existing videos (what they refer to as *tours*). Modifications include adding text, questions, or discussions over the selected videos. Videos are stored directly on the Zaption site. A tutorial can be found here: https://www.youtube.com/watch?v=J-pnOVojYho

FORMATIVE ASSESSMENT TOOLS

As mentioned in Chapter 3, it is essential that teachers consistently check on student understanding both at home and at school to tailor instructional decisions to the needs of their students. Below are descriptions of some of these tools.

Kahoot: This tool, grounded on game-based pedagogy to increase motivation and engagement, allows teachers to create formative assessments and track student responses. Teachers can watch in real time as students respond to questions, either at school or at home. Tutorials and more information can be found here: http://blog.getkahoot.com/tagged/tutorials

Poll Everywhere: This site can be used to create brief open-ended or selected-response quizzes and polls that students can respond to via tablets, computers, and/or cell phones. Although text responses are anonymous, if students create Twitter accounts, it is possible to track individual student data. Here is a brief tutorial: https://www.youtube.com/watch?v=WfgkN2zZIlA

Socrative: Similar in capability to Poll Everywhere, Socrative is a free tool that allows teachers to create digital quizzes, questions, and exit tickets. Teachers can set up accounts that enable them to save or import quizzes, download PDFs of quizzes, and generate reports of student responses. Another interesting feature of this tool is that teachers can assign students to "teams" and have a "space race" based on number of correct responses. A tutorial can be found here: https://www.youtube.com/watch?v=R-4WCq4RZPs

Padlet: Formerly known as "Wallwisher," Padlet is an Internet resource that allows students to post responses to questions by simply double-clicking anywhere on a teacher-created page. The teacher can also add feedback to the page via posts to correct any student errors or misconceptions. Here is a tutorial: https://www.youtube .com/watch?v=bt6orv2QfZw

Evernote: This is a free app that allows users to create notes and organize them based on a topic. There are also tools in this app that allow students to record audio and embed images. After creating a note, students can add audio or images as part of their response and e-mail or tweet them to share with the teacher. A step-by-step tutorial: https://evernote.com/getting_started/

Google Drive: As part of Google's array of tools, Drive allows users to share and edit documents (Docs), respond to polls or surveys (Forms), and engage in live group interactions (Hangout). Docs, in particular, is not only an excellent tool for collaboration among students but also holds a great deal of potential for students interacting virtually with their teachers. Forms allow students to communicate thoughts on their own progress, ideas, questions, and other areas of clarity or confusion with their teacher. This promotes invitation, investment, persistence, and reflection in learning.

Plickers: This free app, available for both Apple and Android devices, allows teachers to gather and save data on student responses to various multiple-choice questions and polls. Students are assigned numbered response cards with four options (A–D), and teachers use the app to record the responses, which are then displayed for the teachers as correct or incorrect, along with percentages. An additional feature allows teachers to use their computers to display results through a projector. An overview and tutorial can be found here: https://plickers.com/help

BACKCHANNELS

Backchannels are essentially virtual chat rooms that teachers can quickly create and monitor. The below resources all enable teachers and students to maintain real-time conversations with each other while other activities are taking place (e.g., interactive lecture, videos, group work), without causing audible disruptions. Although these backchannel resources all serve similar purposes, there are some subtle differences among them so, we suggest exploring each to determine which might best fit your needs. With regard to the differentiated flipped classroom, these tools could serve several purposes, both at home and at school:

At Home

Direct Instruction: Students can split into small groups and schedule their viewing of at-home direct instruction around the same time. The teacher might plan that each group discuss a different question before, during, and/or after the recording (see Chapters 4 and 5 for differentiated questions or prompts based on readiness, interest, and learning profile). Students can share their ideas with each other during this time, and teachers can see the transcript of their work that evening or the next day.

At School

Small Group Activities: Teachers can monitor multiple groups at once by facilitating backchannel conversations while students work in small groups. One member per group can be tasked with synthesizing the group discussions via a backchannel so that the teacher can assess group progress.

Interactive Lectures: Teachers could pause and ask students to respond to prompts or questions at strategically planned times. To differentiate this activity, teachers might have two backchannels going at once with two different prompts adjusted for student readiness (see Chapter 4 for examples of differentiated prompts and questions).

Asking Questions: One concern about flipped instruction is that students do not have the capability to ask questions during direct instruction at home. Backchannel use can help with this as students can post questions as they arise, and these can be addressed the next class.

Monitoring for Respectful Interactions: Teachers can view conversations (in real time or after conversations have ended) to ensure that students are maintaining an appropriate degree of respect when discussing content outside of school.

Here is a list of possible backchannel sites:

Backchannelchat, Chatterous, Chatzy, Google Hangout, and TodaysMeet: Free to use, these resources allows users to create backchannels (or virtual chat rooms) so that students can share comments, questions, or other thoughts in real time. Teachers can moderate these conversations in real time or view transcripts of conversations after conversations have ended.

Twitter: Through use of hashtags to organize tweets, teachers can have students comment via tweets in any of the above scenarios both at home and at school (e.g., #CHSPhysPer2 for Carthage High School second period physics). This is also a free tool.

BLOG SITES

This set of resources can serve numerous educational purposes. As mentioned throughout this book, blogs allow students to keep an online journal and interact through the comment feature on each other's blogs. The following list includes blogs that we have found success with, both within our own classrooms and in the schools where we coach teachers. Again, teachers should devote a few minutes to exploring these resources to determine which are most appropriate and effective for their purposes. It might also be worth polling students to determine whether they are familiar with any of these, and if so, whether they have preferences as to which are implemented.

- LiveJournal
- Kidblog
- Blogster
- Blogger

VARIED LEVELS OF TEXTS

Also discussed in Chapter 4, these sites provide teachers with texts that allow them to differentiate according to reading level or interest while maintaining a common theme.

Booksthatgrow.com: This site provides varied reading levels of the same text. The advantage of this site over the others is that it features well-known texts such as Chechov's *The Bet* and Lincoln's First Inaugural Address. While it offers a wider variety of genre choices (fiction, nonfiction, articles, and essays) than the other sites, it is the only resource on this list that requires a subscription fee.

Commonlit.org: This free resource provides collections of texts on different themes. While it doesn't offer different levels of a *common text* (as do Newsela and Booksthatgrow), it does supply texts of various levels and genres that are united by a *common theme.* This unique feature allows students to read a text on his or her level and contribute insights from that text in a full-group discussion—or to a full group discussion board—around a common essential question (e.g., "How Can Fear be Used to Manipulate?").

Newsela.com: Also a free resource, this unique site presents current event articles on many topics such as science, social studies, arts, and sports, and so on. Each article is offered in five different reading levels so that teachers can assign the level that best suits each student. After reading the article at their level, all students can discuss the same text, either in class or in an electroic forum such as GoogleDocs.

Readworks.org: This free site offers resources to help teachers assign and monitor free-choice books. It presents collections of study guides around common genres (e.g., Fifth-Grade Historical Fiction, Sixth-Grade Science Fiction) to support student choice. Students can select which book they read; teachers can use the resources at this site to infuse accountability and facilitate peer interaction both at home and at school.

Sample Student Technology Survey and School District BYOD Policy

TECHNOLOGY SURVEY

Before attempting to create a differentiated flipped classroom, it is wise to administer a technology survey to determine students' comfort levels and access to key tools that will be used. Although students are living during an intensely technological time, this does not mean that all have access to technology or that they are capable of using it. A survey like the one provided on the following page could help teachers identify potential roadblocks to implementation. In addition to administering this survey, teachers should have a candid discussion with students—and if possible, parents—about the purpose and characteristics of a flipped classroom.

Technology Survey for Ms. Velazquez

1. Do you or a family member/guardian have a computer or tablet at home?

2. Do you or a family member/guardian have a smartphone that you can access on a nightly basis?

3. Do you have access to a DVD player at home?

4. Do you have access to the Internet at home?

If "Yes," skip ahead to Question 7. If "No," continue with Question 5.

5. If you don't have Internet access at home, are you close to a library or some other place (coffee shop, friend's house, fast food restaurant) where you might be able to access it?

6. If you don't have access to the Internet at home, do you have a study hall or some other time during the day when you could watch a brief video and complete an assignment to process that video?

7. What concerns, if any, do you have about viewing "teaching videos" at home?

8. Have any of your past teachers flipped their classrooms? What resources did they use to send content home with you? Did you find those resources easy to use? Explain.

DISTRICTWIDE BYOD POLICY

An often-voiced concern among teachers and administrators involves the use of student devices at school. More and more, schools are embracing the use of student-owned electronic devices (such as smartphones or tablets) for educational purposes through Bring Your Own Devices (BYOD) policies. During more recent school visits, we have noticed a significant increase in schools that have mobile device wireless networks allocated specifically for appropriate BYOD use (e.g., for students to use any devices, they *must* be logged on to that dedicated network). However, it is not enough just to assume students are always adhering to rules of proper use. In addition to classroom policies such as those outlined in Chapter 6, districts often set guidelines for proper BYOD use, as well as consequences should devices be misused. The following policy example, from Harrisonburg City Schools (HCPS) in western Virginia, illustrates how districts can set clear expectations for BYOD use.

Student Use of Personal Electronic Devices

HCPS provides the opportunity for students to bring an electronic device to school to use as an educational tool with parental permission. The use of these electronic devices will be at teacher's discretion.

1. Students must obtain teacher permission before using an electronic device during classroom instruction.

2. Student use of an electronic device must support the instructional activities currently occurring in each classroom and lab and must adhere to the Acceptable Use Agreement.

3. Students must turn off and put away an electronic device when requested by a teacher.

4. Students should be aware that their use of the electronic device could cause distraction for others in the classroom, especially in regard to audio. Therefore, audio should be muted or headphones used when appropriate. Any music would need to be stored on the device and not streamed or downloaded while on the school network.

5. Students may use their personal electronic device before school, at lunch, and after school in adult-supervised areas only, such as the Media Center or classrooms with the teacher present, as long as it does not create a distraction or disruption for others in the area. If an adult asks a student to put his/her electronic device away, the student must comply.

6. Students are NOT permitted to use their personal electronic device to access the Internet by any manner other than connecting through the secure wireless network provided.

SOURCE: Retrieved from http://web.harrisonburg.k12.va.us/tech/docs/tech_plan/Guidelines_Student_Devices.pdf

APPENDIX C

Interest and Learning Profile Task Examples

C.1 JIGSAW: POLYNOMIALS

Standard:

CCSS.MATH.CONTENT.6.EE.A.2

Write, read, and evaluate expressions in which letters stand for numbers.

Learning Goals:

Understanding:

- Students will understand that like terms have the same variable and degree.

Knowledge:

- The distributive property.
- The steps of adding polynomials.
- The steps of subtracting polynomials.
- The steps of multiplying polynomials.

Skills:

- Add polynomials.
- Subtracting polynomials.
- Multiplying a polynomial by a monomial.
- Multiply polynomials.
- Apply the proper theorems to the equations (Remainder, Binomial, etc.).
- Use polynomials to describe numerical relationships.

Jigsaw Task Introduction (Home Groups)

Teacher asks students to come up with definitions of "polynomial" and "monomial" within their home groups. After using those student-generated definitions to make a few introductory remarks, the teacher presents the different section titles and students will select which section they want to work with.

Expert Group 1	Expert Group 2	Expert Group 3	Expert Group 4
Section 8–5 (Part 1) Adding Polynomials	Section 8–5 (Part 2) Subtracting Polynomials	Section 8–6 Multiplying a Polynomial by a Monomial	Section 8–7 Multiplying Polynomials

Expert Group Understanding Check

Students will explore their topic by watching videos on Khan Academy (or if technology is not available, they can use textbooks). As a group they will fill out the questionnaire in a Google Doc, which includes:

1. What vocabulary is necessary to know for this topic? Provide a description/definition for each.
2. Steps with explanation (describe each step).
3. Multiple strategies for solving with explanation of each.
4. Helpful hints.
5. Example problems (at least 3).

(Continued)

(Continued)

Home Group Synthesis/Sharing Task

Students return to their home group where they each share their topic in order of the sections. Each person will share his or her vocabulary terms, steps for the problem, multiple strategies, and demonstrate an example problem for the group. They will also provide helpful hints and give the group its own problem and check for correctness when everyone is finished. Students will use take their own notes while each group member is presenting his or her topic. When the presenter is done students will ask any remaining questions they have and look for patterns and connections within the topic or to another topic.

Home Group Accountability

Each group receives four questions (one from each topic). They will be asked to solve them as a group. The person who presented the topic will write down the steps and the answer while the presenter's fellow group members explain the steps and tell the presenter what to write. This collaborative step will prepare them for the final individual understanding check.

Individual Understanding Check

Students will have an exit card where they solve four problems (one from each topic). Then they are to describe the process and steps for solving one type of problem (that type of problem must be different from their own topic).

Whole Class Discussion/Sharing

Students will be asked to provide the patterns and connections they noticed within the topics and between different topics.

Rubric

	2 Points	1 Point	0 Points
Vocabulary	All necessary vocabulary terms are provided and described correctly and in-depth.	Vocabulary definitions are not descriptive. Missing one or two necessary terms.	Missing many necessary terms. Definitions not provided.
Steps	All steps are included with explanations of each step.	Most steps are included with unclear explanations.	Only a couple of steps provided with no explanation.
Multiple Strategies	Many (two or more) strategies for solving the problem are provided with an in-depth description of each.	Two or more strategies are provided for solving the problem but there is no description of the less used strategies.	Only one strategy is provided.
Example Problems	Example problems are correct with clear steps for others to follow.	Example problem is correct but does not have clear steps to follow.	Example problems are incorrect and work is not shown.
Helpful Hints	Two to three helpful hints that make the problems and process easier to understand.	One or two helpful hints that don't apply to problem much or don't help clarify anything in the problem.	No helpful hints provided.

SOURCE: Used with permission of Katie O'Brien; Jigsaw Format from Doubet & Hockett, 2015.

C.2A   RAFT: RELATIONS AND FUNCTIONS

Standard:
CCSS.MATH.CONTENT.HSF.BF.A.1
Write a function that describes a relationship between two quantities.

Learning Goals:

Understanding:

- Students will understand that relationships exist and define many things (in math)

Knowledge:

- Relation between inputs/outputs
- Vertical line test

Skills:

- Test whether a relation is a function or not
- Convert relations and functions into different forms (ordered pairs, diagram, etc.)

This RAFT is differentiated for student:	Evaluation Criteria (see attached rubric):
☑ Interest	Mathematical Content, Mathematical Accuracy, Mechanics

This RAFT is a(n)	When and how this RAFT will be used:
☑ Sense-making activity ☑ Assessment	This RAFT will be used for in-class practice after students watch at-home content on relations and functions (the basic features) and how to write/read them in different forms such as in ordered pair form or in graph form. They will also incorporate their prior knowledge of how to distinguish a regular relation and a relation that is also a function.

Role	Audience	Format	Topic
Inputs	Outputs	An Illustrated Note	DTR: Determine the Relationship
Vertical Line	Function Police	A Police Report	Written description of a relation caught as a repeat offender
Function	Superhero Academy	A Student Application	Essay portion of an application where you describe your special ability to change forms
You right now as a relation	You in the future as a function	A Letter (from the future)	A letter written to yourself in the past describing how you must change from a relation to a function in order to save the world!

Task Cards

Input: You are a set of inputs and you are writing a note to a special (ooh la la) set of outputs. You two are very much connected and have been so for a very long time, so it's about time you "Determine the Relationship." You must describe the elements in your set and how they relate to the elements in the output's set of elements, using any relationship/pattern rule that you would like. To further express your feelings, you must display the special relationship (pattern/rule) that connects you (inputs) to the outputs in whatever form you desire.

Vertical Line: You are a vertical line police officer out to round up all the rowdy, nonfunctions in your town. You have come across a suspicious relation and must write up a police report describing the features of the relation and how you know that it is not a function. It's your duty to put away this repeat offender!

Function: You are a function looking to enroll in the famous Superhero Academy. The admission process requires an application that includes an essay. In that essay, you must describe your special form-changing powers that you think qualify you to join the Superhero Academy. Be very specific about the forms you can take on and what those looks like for your unique inputs and outputs! It's time to wow the admissions office!

Yourself (relation): You are a famous function—the function that saved the world! You must write a letter to yourself in the past, when you were only a young, naïve relation, telling yourself how you turned from being a relation into a function. Be very detailed about the things that are different between the you now (function) and the you back then (relation) so that you will know exactly what to do so that you can become the world-saving function that you grew up to be!

Rubric

	3 Points	2 Points	1 Point
Mathematical Content	Students include all of the points described in the prompt and are clear or detailed about the point they are trying to make—the details they include work to support the final conclusion from the prompt.	Students include all or most of the points described in the prompt but are not clear or detailed about the point they are trying to make—the details they include are not clearly related to the final conclusion from the prompt.	Students include only some of the points described in the prompt and are not clear about the point they are trying to make—the details they include are not coherent or supportive to the final conclusion from the prompt.
Mathematical Accuracy	Students describe and discuss the features and properties of functions and relations correctly and coherently. Students accurately describe the distinction between relations and functions.	Students describe and discuss the features and properties of functions and relations in a slightly incoherent, disorderly manner but are on the right track. Students have a general sense of the distinction between relations and functions.	Students did not describe and discuss the features and properties of functions and relations coherently and also included many mistakes in mathematical reasoning. Students are not clear on the distinction between relations and functions.
Mechanics	Students wrote in an organized, logical manner with appropriate length (more than a few sentences). There were few spelling and grammar mistakes.	Students wrote in a somewhat disorganized manner or with inappropriate length (only a few sentences). There were some spelling and grammar mistakes.	Students wrote in a disorganized, unclear manner with inappropriate length (only than a few sentences). There were several spelling and grammar mistakes.

SOURCE: Used with permission of Beth Kent; RAFT Format from Doubet & Hockett, 2015.

Goals: The student will investigate and understand how the world manages renewable and nonrenewable resources.

Standards:

NGSS: 4-ESS3-1

Obtain and combine information to describe that energy and fuels are derived from natural resources and their uses affect the environment.

- *ESS 3.A: Natural Resources*
  - O *Energy and fuels that humans use are derived from natural sources, and their use affects the environment in multiple ways. Some resources are renewable over time, and others are not.*

Understanding:

- Students will understand that conservation means using our resources wisely and protecting them for the future.
- Students will understand that conservation of resources and environmental protection begin with individual acts of stewardship.

Knowledge:

- Resources can be recycled and reused in various formats.
- Pollution prevention and waste management are less costly than cleanup.

Skills: Students will be able to

- Describe the different methods of reusing and recycling resources
- Determine the results of proper and improper acts of stewardship
- Analyze cost/benefit resource use options in everyday activities

This RAFT is differentiated for student:	Evaluation Criteria (see rubric):
☑ Interest	1. Content 2. Accuracy 3. Organization 4. Editing and Publishing
This RAFT is a(n) ☑ Anchor Activity for conservation Unit ☑ Sense-making activity ☑ Jigsaw Task	**When and how this RAFT will be used:** 1. After studying types of renewable and nonrenewable resources, students will be allowed to choose which RAFT they want to complete. Students will submit their top two choices on an index card, and the teacher will use those choices to assign groups (4 students per group). 2. Groups of four students working on the same option will receive a task card and complete the task as outlined in the instructions. This work will be completed as "anchor activity" work at school while the class progresses through the rest of the unit. Since groups are working in Google Docs and can therefore collaborate at home, this work will also serve as homework several nights, 3. At the end of the unit—and before the test—students will regroup into mixed groups with all options represented, share products, and discuss the similar individual acts of stewardship each option shares. This will serve as a test review.

Role	Audience	Format	Topic
Architect	Board Members	Blueprint	"Proposal to build your new 'Green' headquarters."
Polar Bear	Humans	Petition	"Look at what your trash is doing to my home."
Fashion Designer	Style Magazine Readers	Magazine Spread	"Who used it better? What to do—or *not* to do—with your old clothes and accessories."
Travel Agent	Vacationers	Brochure	"Sit back and relax! Visit scenic _____ to learn and partake of our native conservation traditions."

Architect: You will assume the role of an architect who has been hired by _____ (your choice of major industry in our community) to design a new and improved "green" version of their facility. Your duty is to produce a blueprint of your building. Your blueprint must include

- a sketch of the building design;
- a list of two minimum recycled building materials you plan to use and why (cost efficiency, impact on environment, longevity); and
- a list of three minimum "green" design aspects of the building; explain why these accommodations conserve or reduce waste of resources.

You must use our textbook, your notes, and reliable online resources (review the "EvaluatingWebsites" tutorial: http://ed.ted.com/on/TPQmKnKq).

Polar Bear: You are one angry polar bear who is fed up with your habitat unprotected. Your task is to write a petition to send to the human population explaining how their poor resource management skills are affecting your life. Your petition must include

- at least 3 examples of pollution occurring in your environment, explain what the sources/causes of these pollutants are;
- at least 2 suggestions for how humans can prevent pollution and promote conservation in your habitat; and
- potential consequences your habitat will suffer if humans fail to listen to your petition.

You must use our textbook, your notes, and reliable online resources (review the "EvaluatingWebsites" tutorial: http://ed.ted.com/on/TPQmKnKq).

Fashion Designer: You are the next Miranda Priestly, Editor in chief of *Style* magazine. Your upcoming issue features a spread on what to do with old clothes and accessories. Your two-page spread must include

- 3 examples of dos when managing clothing and accessory materials,
- 3 examples of don'ts when managing clothing and accessory materials, and
- suggestions of durable and eco-friendly fabrics readers should be encouraged to purchase in the future and why.

You must use our textbook, your notes, and reliable online resources (review the "EvaluatingWebsites" tutorial: http://ed.ted.com/on/TPQmKnKq).

Travel Agent: You were just hired by a remote vacation location to advertise the natives' beautiful land and how they take care of it. Your task is to produce a three-panel brochure to encourage vacationers to visit the land to partake of a meaningful yet relaxing vacation. Your brochure must include

- a brief history of the land including what renewable and nonrenewable resources are available,
- a description of where the vacationers can stay and what food options are available, and
- 3 vacation activities that relate to the experiential learning of how the land manages their resources.

You must use our textbook, your notes, and reliable online resources (review the "EvaluatingWebsites" tutorial: http://ed.ted.com/on/TPQmKnKq).

Closure Activity

1. Multiple copies of projects will be made for each student in each group to keep and share with their mixed groups.

2. Students will be placed in mixed groups to share their projects, four members in each group representing each of the different projects.

3. Once students share each of their projects, they will have a discussion in each of their groups about the importance of stewardship.

4. In the mixed groups, students will develop a list of guidelines for how individuals can act with stewardship.

5. The groups will share their lists in a whole class discussion—either in class or online. The following questions can be utilized to guide the discussion:

   a. What acts of stewardship can we do all do right now?

   b. Why is prevention of waste more desirable than management of waste?

   c. Why do we take proactive approaches to manage resources? What could happen if we don't?

SOURCE: Used with permission of Jenny Lewinski; RAFT Format from Doubet & Hockett, 2015.

Rubric

Categories	Proposal Accepted	Proposal Considered	Proposal Returned
Content	Your product addresses all of the following learning goals: • Resources can be recycled and reused in various formats • Pollution prevention and waste management are less costly than cleanup • Describe the different methods of reusing and recycling resources • Determine the results of proper and improper acts of stewardship • Analyze cost/benefit resource use options in everyday activities	Your product fails to address one or two of the following learning goals: • Resources can be recycled and reused in various formats • Pollution prevention and waste management are less costly than cleanup • Describe the different methods of reusing and recycling resources • Determine the results of proper and improper acts of stewardship • Analyze cost/benefit resource use options in everyday activities	Your product fails to address three or more of the following learning goals: • Resources can be recycled and reused in various formats • Pollution prevention and waste management are less costly than cleanup • Describe the different methods of reusing and recycling resources • Determine the results of proper and improper acts of stewardship • Analyze cost/benefit resource use options in everyday activities
Clarity	All questions raised in the task card were addressed correctly and in detail. The finished project was filled with information necessary to get the point across.	The content was correct, but was missing some aspects that would have made the finished product a better reflection of the scientific content.	The content was incorrect and incomplete. There were several errors that took away from the finished product. More detail was needed to reflect the scientific content.
Accuracy	All explanations and examples were factually correct, drawn from reputable sources, and appropriately illustrated and explained.	Most explanations and examples were factually correct and were factually correct, drawn from reputable sources, and appropriately illustrated/explained.	Most explanations and examples were neither factually correct, drawn from reputable sources, nor appropriately illustrated/explained.
Editing and Publishing	The final product was presented well and the organization contributed to the overall success of the product communicating the management and use of resources. The product is virtually error free and ready to be shared with the world!	The organization communicated the point for the most part, but portions were confusing and needed to be reread to fully understand the management and use of resources. There were little to no grammatical mistakes. Minor editing is required to reach perfection!	There was little organization on the finished project. The information appears compiled without regard to effectively communicating the point. There were numerous grammatical mistakes. Major revisions are needed before this product will be ready to share with others.

This learning menu will be used as a sense-making/anchor activity supplement throughout a unit on persuasive techniques in media. After introductions, lectures, and explanations for a specific lesson—delivered both at home and at school—students will be instructed to work on specific and corresponding portions of this learning menu—both at home and at school. Side dishes and desserts can be completed when assigned class work is finished at school. These menu choices will allow students to demonstrate whether or not they are grasping the learning goals outlined below.

Standard:

CCSS.ELA-LITERACY.SL.8.2

Analyze the purpose of information presented in diverse media and formats (e.g., visually, quantitatively, orally) and evaluate the motives (e.g., social, commercial, political) behind its presentation.

Understandings for All Courses:

- Students will understand that persuasive techniques are intentional choices designed to produce a desired effect on an audience.

Main Dish Knowledge:

- Definition of key types of persuasive techniques

Main Dish Skills:

- Analyze media to identify different persuasive techniques
- Determine purpose of media message and its effect on an audience

Side Dish Skills:

- Use persuasive techniques to convince an audience of intended purpose

Desserts provide extensions of Main Dish Knowledge and Skills

Appetizer (each student must complete the following):

- You will select one of the following three video advertisements to watch. Each of these videos uses persuasive techniques. Watch video individually and answer the following questions:

  o What is the purpose of this video advertisement?
  o What tools are used within this video in terms of persuasion?
  o How does this video make you feel as a viewer?

Video Options:

1. https://www.youtube.com/watch?v=pTjHCCU2E4c (Google Chrome)
2. https://www.youtube.com/watch?v=-c4MNWLtSS8 (Boost Mobile Cell Phone)
3. https://www.youtube.com/watch?v=ZmBDeswu2dl (Diet Coke)

We will discuss your findings as a class once everyone has completed this portion of the menu.

Main Dishes (Each student must complete every activity listed below during time assigned by teacher):

- You will be assigned to a group that will be given a persuasive technique of *ethos, pathos, or logos* (remember these are the techniques we have just learned today).

- Within your group, it is your job to use the persuasive technique you were assigned to create and act out a short ad that will make your audience (the rest of the class) want to buy your product (product of your choice; get product approved by me).

- Each group will create a short write-up on their ad detailing:

  o What technique they are representing

  o How they are representing the technique

  o Why their ad is effective

- Each group will present their ad to the class, and it is up to the viewers to <u>analyze and decide which technique is being used</u> and if it was <u>effective in its purpose</u> of persuading us to buy the product.

Main Dish Jigsaw: (*Teacher Note:* This allows for readiness differentiation through specific grouping based on readiness and persuasive terms assigned based on readiness levels.)

The rest of the main dishes will be completed in the form of a jigsaw. You will be assigned a certain persuasive technique and, using Google Docs, will join up with your group members that are assigned the same technique to complete the following, both at home and at school:

1. Define your assigned technique (bandwagon, snob appeal, bribery, humor, testimonial, or association).

2. Give an example (written explanation) of this technique that we would see in our everyday lives.

3. Find an example of this technique used in media (television, radio, magazines, newspapers, etc.). Analyze and write down the purpose of your selected example and the effect it has on its audience.

4. Come back to your home groups and share what you have found with group members. Students should fill out the following graphic organizer with information given about each technique.

Side Dishes (Choose one of the following activities to complete. You may collaborate with others who chose the same option. While you are expected to use menu time to begin your work, you can continue it at home, if you so choose.):

1. Create a **billboard/illustration** that exemplifies a <u>persuasive technique</u> of your choice to convince your audience of something. The persuasive technique can be chosen from the ones we have gone over so far throughout this unit. Make sure to identify the technique(s) you use. This billboard can be persuading someone on a topic of your choice.

2. Create a **video commercial** that exemplifies a <u>persuasive technique</u> of your choice to convince your audience of something. The persuasive technique can be chosen from the ones we have gone over so far throughout this unit. Make sure to identify the technique(s) you use. This commercial can be persuading someone on a topic of your choice.

3. Create a **radio advertisement** that exemplifies a <u>persuasive technique</u> of your choice to convince your audience of something. The persuasive technique can be chosen from the ones we have gone over so far throughout this unit. Make sure to identify the technique(s) you use. This radio advertisement can be persuading someone on a topic of your choice.

(Continued)

(Continued)

4. Create a **newspaper/magazine** article that exemplifies a <u>persuasive technique</u> of your choice to convince your audience of something. The persuasive technique can be chosen from the ones we have gone over so far throughout this unit. Make sure to identify the technique(s) you use. This newspaper/magazine article can be persuading someone on a topic of your choice.

Desserts (Complete as many as you have time to complete during designated menu time):

1. Research a persuasive technique we have not covered as a class.

   o Explain the technique's purpose.
   o Find a media example of this technique that you can share to inform the rest of the class about this new technique.

2. Look up advertisement from the past (at least 10 years ago).

   o How do these advertisements' use of persuasive techniques compare to those used today?
   o Were these advertisements more or less effective than the ones we see today?
   o Explain why.

3. What do you think is the least useful persuasive technique?

   o Provide explanation of your thinking.
   o Provide an example of how this persuasive technique is not very useful.
   o Could this "least effective" technique be combined with other persuasive techniques to make it more effective? Explain.

Main Dish Jigsaw Organizer

Persuasive Technique	Definition	Example From Everyday Life	Description of Media Example
Bandwagon			
Snob Appeal			
Bribery			
Humor			
Testimonial			
Association			

SOURCE: Used with permission of Megan Richard; Learning Menu Format from Doubet & Hockett, 2015.

THE DIFFERENTIATED FLIPPED CLASSROOM

Rubric

Categories	Expert	Developing	Needs Improvement
Main Dish (Ad Skit)	Ad Topic: ____ Ad is representative of assigned persuasive technique, including all its shades of meaning • Ethos • Pathos • Logos Ad demonstrates nuanced ability to determine the purpose of media message and its effect on the audience Ad presents convincing case that will compel viewers to buy product Write-up of ad presents accurate conception of and clear insight into use of persuasive terms: • ____ persuasive technique used and provides accurate definition • ____ includes evidence and reasoning behind how you are representing the persuasive technique	Ad Topic: ____ Ad is representative of assigned persuasive technique in a concrete, one-dimensional way • Ethos • Pathos • Logos Ad demonstrates concrete ability to determine the purpose of media message and its effect on the audience Ad presents a clear case that might compel viewers to buy product Write-up of ad presents accurate conception of and limited insight into use of persuasive terms: • ____ persuasive technique used and provides accurate definition • ____ includes evidence and reasoning behind how you are representing the persuasive technique	Ad Topic: ____ Ad is not fully representative of assigned persuasive technique • Ethos • Pathos • Logos Ad demonstrates limited ability to determine the purpose of media message and its effect on the audience Ad presents an unclear case that is not likely to compel viewers to buy product Write-up of ad presents inaccurate conception of and limited insight into use of persuasive terms: • ____ persuasive technique used and provides accurate definition • ____ includes evidence and reasoning behind how you are representing the persuasive technique

(Continued)

Categories	Expert	Developing	Needs Improvement
Main Dish (Jigsaw)	Graphic Organizer is accurately/insightfully completed • Accurately defined technique • Discussion of ways specific persuasive techniques are seen in everyday life • Crystallizing example of how these techniques are seen in everyday life • Media example with analysis of purpose and effect on audience	Graphic Organizer lacks one of the following: • Accurately defined technique • Discussion of ways specific persuasive techniques are seen in everyday life • Crystallizing example of how these techniques are seen in everyday life • Media example with analysis of purpose and effect on audience	Graphic Organizer lacks two or more of the following: • Accurately defined technique • Discussion of ways specific persuasive techniques are seen in everyday life • Crystallizing example of how these techniques are seen in everyday life • Media example with analysis of purpose and effect on audience
Side Dishes	Provides context necessary to fully understand topic Analysis of your finished product provides detailed and specific explanation of how the product exemplifies your chosen technique Product thoroughly convinces audience of intended purpose Finished product's quality (appearance and conventions) enhances persuasive appeal	Provides context that hints at topic's background Analysis of your finished product provides general explanation of how the product exemplifies your chosen technique Product convinces audience of intended purpose Finished product's quality (appearance and conventions) does not detract from persuasive appeal	Fails to provide context necessary to understand topic Analysis of your finished product does not support how the product exemplifies your chosen technique Product fails to convince audience of intended purpose Finished product's quality (appearance and conventions) detracts from persuasive appeal
Dessert	Provides insightful explanation of the persuasive techniques' purpose Analyzes media to identify nuanced persuasive techniques Gives detailed explanations for all questions	Provides clear explanation of the persuasive techniques' purpose Analyzes media to identify obvious persuasive techniques Gives general explanations for all questions	Provides unclear explanation of the persuasive techniques' purpose Analysis misses persuasive techniques used in media Gives insufficient explanations for all questions

C.3B LEARNING MENU: AMERICAN CULTURE IN THE 1920–1930s

Unit Topic: 1920s–1930s in America
Standard:
CCSS.ELA-LITERACY.RH.9-10.3   *Analyze in detail a series of events described in a text; determine whether earlier events caused later ones or simply preceded them.*

Understanding:

- Students will understand that cultures are dynamic and change over time.

Knowledge:

- Norms and values in American culture changed after World War I (Prohibition, women's suffrage, traditional religion, and Darwin's theory)

- News mediums of mass communication (radio, magazines, movies) that still influence popular culture today emerged in 1920s America

- The overarching causes of the Great Depression (Stock Market Crash of 1929, Collapse of national banking system and the Federal Reserve, decline of world trade, and the Smoot-Hawley Act)

- The Great Depression caused unemployment, homelessness, political unrest, and farm foreclosures.

Skills:

- Relate American literature to domestic life in the 1920s and 1930s.

- Compare and contrast different time periods.

- Evaluate how historical events cause cultural changes.

Task Introduction and Implementation (Teacher's Note):

The learning menu will be given to students at the beginning of our 1920s–1930s in America unit. On the introduction day of the unit, we will explore the learning menu as a class and students will have the opportunity to ask any initial questions. The menu will be used as a performance assessment and turned in at the end of the unit. In addition to designated at-home and at-school assignments, students will use the menu as an anchor activity and work on it when they finish assignments early in class. All the readings, materials, and resources will be located in the class Dropbox online. Students will be evaluated on content knowledge and historical literacy skills. To keep their work together, all students will put together a folder with their work compiled.

Appetizers (choose one):

1. 1920s Versus Present-Day Media

At home, watch "1920s Media" (https://www.youtube.com/watch?v=V1ONk_W0zTc). While watching the video, study the different media used (see the second knowledge goal) in the 1920s and 1930s. After watching the video, create a Venn Diagram comparing mass media in the 1920s–1930s and mass media used today. Explain what is the same, what is different, and talk about how mass media would be different in your life. These should be written in complete sentences, not one or two words!!

(Continued)

(Continued)

2. NY Times Article

You are a journalist for the *New York Times* in present day. At home, watch "10 Facts about Television" (https://www.youtube.com/watch?v=ldX-KVT6hh0) and study the pictures on the sheet titled "Modern Day Communication" located in our class Dropbox. Write a column on changes in mass communication (see the second knowledge goal) and describe how these changes have impacted our society. Then create a "letter to the editor" (a short paragraph) as someone who thinks that these media have not changed significantly. The "letter" should explain your reasoning.

Side Dishes (choose one):

1. Freeze Frames

Working in a group of four to five, you will create and perform four freeze frames in front of the class. Use any of the props in the class resource bucket to reenact scenes comparing modern-day social life to society during the Roaring 20s and the Great Depression. Remember the rules of freeze frame: no talking while you act out your scene, freeze when the teacher "pauses" the scene, and be prepared to answer questions about the scene when you are "poked" by your teacher and/or classmates. Feel free to add music to your scene choices—but be prepared to justify your musical choices and keep it school-appropriate!!

2. "The Story of My Life"

You are a radio DJ working on a national heritage project—you are going to use modern music to teach radio listeners about American history. Using modern music, create a playlist with a minimum of seven songs. These songs should have music and lyrics that describe what life was like during the Roaring Twenties and/or the Great Depression. For each song, list the song title and artist. Also include a one- to two-sentence description of how the song fits into the era. All songs must be school-appropriate!!

(Example: "Shake It Off" by Taylor Swift—"Shake It Off" is a fast-paced anthem about girls who act independently and do not care what others think about them. The lyrics describe many changes for young females when they socialized at night and during the weekends. During the 1920s, women started to "stay out too late" and "go on too many dates," according to the older generations.)

Main Dishes (complete all):

1. Society in Novels

Read the excerpts from *The Great Gatsby* and *Of Mice and Men*. The first novel takes place prior to the Great Depression, and the second is set during the Great Depression. Write a paragraph describing the social life in each novel. Answer the following questions: What did the characters do in their free time? What did they eat and drink? Compare the settings of the two stories. How does this compare to society in the 1920s–1930s we discussed in class?

2. Cause-and-Effect Chart

Read the article titled "Events that Caused the Great Depression." Use the activity chart in Dropbox and follow the directions on the activity sheet to organize FIVE important causes of the Great Depression cause-and-effect chart. In the left column, list a cause of the Depression. In the middle column, list the reasons for the cause. Why did the event(s) happen? In the right-hand column, write the effects of the event(s). What happened as a result? This column is a chance for you to justify your choices—why did this have such an impact and why was it a major cause of the Depression?

3. American Filmstrip

You are the director of an upcoming film focused on culture in the 1920s. To plan out your film, create a frame-by-frame outline depicting how a particular social issue changed in 1920s America. You can focus on one of the following: women's suffrage, public opinion on traditional religion, or Prohibition—or focus on another social change you believe was important during the 1920s (ask me prior to starting). Each frame should show a specific "scene" that shows the audience how it changed society. Scene 1 should show what society was like before the events, and scenes 2–4 should show the effects of this change. Follow the template in the Dropbox.

Desserts (complete as many as you have time for—anchor activities and menu time):

1. Great Depression Photojournalism

You are a photojournalist traveling throughout the United States during the Great Depression. Use the PowerPoint slides of the Great Depression located in our class Dropbox to study primary source images from that time period. Each photo is labeled Image 1 through Image 7. Using the image number for each photo, write a caption that will be published in a national newspaper. Each caption should be a single sentence, encompassing the situation and emotions of the subject of the photo (Hint: Think of the effects of the Great Depression listed above our learning goals).

2. Great Depression Children's Book

You have been hired by a children's author to draw pictures about the Great Depression. Using the secondary document written by PBS, "The Great Depression," create four different illustrations with captions to explain the causes of the Great Depression to elementary school students.

3. The Roaring Twenties Day in the Life

Pick a perspective of a teenager living in the 1920s. Using at least 10 school-appropriate 1920s slang words, write a diary entry describing your day. You stories should be a minimum of five sentences in length and focus on a specific event/change in society (see the knowledge learning goals: prohibition, women's suffrage, Darwin's Theory). In your diary entry, I should be able to identify your perspective, and your opinions should be backed with evidence from our textbook and class notes.

Sources

Fitzgerald, F. S. (1925). *The great Gatsby*. Retrieved from https://ebooks.adelaide.edu .au/f/fitzgerald/f_scott/gatsby/contents.html

Krawetz, D. *Unit: The Great Depression and the New Deal* [Word document]. Retrieved from class website: www.africanafrican.com/folder12/.../gr8_great_depress_pt1.doc

Library of Congress. (Updated 2014). *The Great Depression: Collection connections* [photography files]. Retrieved from http://www.loc.gov/teachers/classroommaterials/ themes/great-depression/collections.html

Public Broadcasting Service. (n.d.). *The Great Depression*. Retrieved from http://www.pbs .org/wgbh/americanexperience/features/general-article/dustbowl-great-depression/

Steinbeck, J. (1937). *Of mice and men*. Retrieved from http://www.kgbsd.org/cms/lib3/ AK01001769/Centricity/Domain/664/Of_Mice_and_ Men_-_Full_Text.pdf

....

SOURCE: Used with permission of Danielle Brookover; Learning Menu Format from Doubet & Hockett, 2015.

Rubric

	Expert	Developing	Needs Improvement	
Appetizer	• Used factually correct information • Described the similarities and differences between 1920s–1930s media and modern-day media • Discussed the impact of media on society • Followed assignment directions	• Used factually correct information • Described the similarities and differences between 1920s–1930s media and modern-day media • Did not discuss the impact of media on society • Followed assignment directions	• May or may not have used factually correct information • Did not describe similarities or differences between 1920s–1930s media and modern-day media • Did not discuss the impact of media on society • May or may not have followed assignment directions	
Feedback (For each course, this section will be used to write in feedback and explain students' scores to them.)				
Side Dishes	• Students proficiently explained or justified their scenes or song choices • Students strongly connected their scene or song choices to the 1920s–1930s • Student scene or song choices used factually correct information	• Students adequately explained or justified their scenes or song choices • Students connected their scene or song choices to the 1920s–1930s • Student scene or song choices used factually correct information	• Students did not explain or justify their scenes or song choices • Students did not connect their scene or song choices to the 1920s–1930s • Student scene or song choices were not factually correct or pertaining to the era	
Feedback				

	Expert	Developing	Needs Improvement

Main Dish: Society in Novels	• Paragraph successfully explained all necessary components:
	  ○ Descriptions of the characters and setting of the novels
	  ○ Compared the settings of both novels
	  ○ Related the novels to the content discussed about the 1920s–1930s society in class
	
	• Students used quotes from the novels as evidence
	• Followed directions for the activity
		• Paragraph adequately explained most of the necessary components:
		  ○ Descriptions of the characters and setting of the novels
		  ○ Students either compared the settings of both novels or relate the novels to the content discussed about the 1920s–1930s in class
		
		• Students paraphrased the novel
		• Followed directions for activity
			• Students did not write a paragraph
			• Students wrote a paragraph that did not explain the necessary components
			  ○ Students may not have described the characters and setting
			  ○ Students did not compare the settings or related the novels to 1920s–1930s society
			• Students did not reference the novel in their paragraph
			• Student may not have followed directions

Feedback			
Main Dish: Cause-and-Effect Chart	• Listed factually accurate information causes of the Great Depression • Described the reasons for the cause • Described the impact during/ after the Great Depression	• Listed factually accurate information—the causes of the Great Depression • Listed the reasons for the cause • Attempted to but did not describe the impact	• May or may not have listed factually accurate information—the causes of the Great Depression • May or may not have listed reasons for the cause • Did not describe the impact
Feedback			

(Continued)

	Expert	Developing	Needs Improvement
Main Dish: American Filmstrip	• Described the changes in society in both picture and word form • Described more than one social change in the 1920s • Described a vivid picture of 1920s society • Followed directions for activity	• Described the changes in society in both picture and word form • Described at least one social change in the 1920s • Described an accurate picture of 1920s society • Followed directions for activity	• Did not describe the changes in society in both picture and word form • Described one or no social changes • Described an incomplete or inaccurate picture of 1920s society • Did not follow directions for activity
Feedback			
Desserts	• Content is factually accurate • Options 1 and 2: in-depth descriptions of different ways society was impacted by the causes of the Depression • Option 3: strong connection to the impact of changes in society to a teenager's life • Followed directions for chosen assignments	• Content is mostly accurate • Options 1 and 2: adequate descriptions of different ways society was impacted by the causes of the Depression • Option 3: attempted or small connection to the impact of changes in society to a person's life • Followed directions for chosen assignments	• Content is not factually accurate or incomplete • Options 1 and 2: Missing components and little attempt to describe the impact of the Depression on society • Option 3: Several missing components of the assignment, which limited the connections to changes in society made • Did not follow directions or did not complete chosen assignments
Feedback			

Standards:

CCSS.ELA-LITERACY.RL.9-10.2

Determine a theme or central idea of a text and analyze in detail its development over the course of the text, including how it emerges and is shaped and refined by specific details; provide an objective summary of the text.

CCSS.ELA-LITERACY.W.9-10.1

Write arguments to support claims in an analysis of substantive topics or texts, using valid reasoning and relevant and sufficient evidence.

Understanding:

- Students will understand that language can be used to influence the perspectives and opinions of others.

Knowledge:

- The themes in the classic *1984* (threats of strict governments, social disorder, psychological manipulation, filtering of information, and the use of technology as a weapon).
- Persuasive techniques (repetition, emotional appeal, logical appeal, anecdote, rhetorical question, statistics, etc.).

Skills:

- Compare the development of themes in multiple pieces of literature
- Provide textual evidence to detail the emergence of a theme in literature
- Present cohesive argument regarding theme using reasoning, technique, and evidence

Task Options (Choose One)		
Analytical	**Practical**	**Creative**
You have read *1984* in your English class. You believe there is a more current young adult novel next year's students could read that could take the place of *1984* but still cover the same themes your teacher discussed in class. To replace *1984* with the novel of your choice, you must present your argument to the English department in your school. • Review the list of themes discussed in class and research young adult novels that portray these themes.	You write for a popular blog site about the latest blockbusters, restaurants, and books, among other topics. You have just finished reading *1984* and really enjoyed it, but you couldn't help noticing how some of the themes paralleled another young adult novel you just read. You decided to write an "If You Like This, You'll Love . . ." column as your next blog post that explains why readers who love *1984* will also love a young adult novel of your choice. • Decide on at least two themes (discussed	You have just read *1984*. There is a rumor around Hollywood that a new film adaptation of the novel is in the works. However, you see many of the same themes from *1984* in another young adult novel. As a result, you believe the film industry would be better served by instead making the young adult novel into a film that parallels *1984*. Create a storyboard of a few key scenes to present as a proposal to the film industry. • Decide on at least two themes (discussed in

(Continued)

(Continued)

- Choose a young adult novel that includes a majority of the themes present in *1984* (pick at least two themes).
- Create a formal presentation with a visual that compares the two novels to make your argument more compelling.
- Outline the themes you choose and use textual evidence to support those themes
- Use at least three persuasive techniques in your presentation to support your argument.

in class) that are comparable in both novels.

- Write the column for your blog that expresses your opinion and persuades people to read the novel you chose.
- Be sure to include two themes along with textual evidence to support those themes
- Write article in an informal journalistic style that uses three persuasive techniques that would connect with today's blog readers.

class) that are reflected in both the *1984* and your film adaptation.

- Create a storyboard of at least two key scenes; each must include at least five frames and important textual evidence and context to provide support.
- For each scene, write an explanation persuading the filmmakers why these scenes reflect themes in *1984* using at least three persuasive techniques.

Closure Activity

Students will present their projects in groups of students with different tasks. After students have presented, they will compare their projects and find similarities between the different products. Students will participate in an online Kidblog discussion explaining which novel they were most persuaded to read in place of or in addition to *1984* and why. In addition to writing their own post, students must comment on three classmates' choices.

Rubric

	Expert	Well-Developed	Needs Improvement
Themes _____ /20	Student addresses at least two of the following: • Threats of strict governments • Social disorder • Psychological manipulation • Filtering of information • Use of technology as a weapon Both themes are thoroughly connected to 1984 and the young adult novel.	Student addresses at least two of the following: • Threats of strict governments • Social disorder • Psychological manipulation • Filtering of information • Use of technology as a weapon Minor problems connecting one or more themes from 1984 with the young adult novel.	Student addresses one or fewer of the following: • Threats of strict governments • Social disorder • Psychological manipulation • Filtering of information • Use of technology as a weapon Major problems connecting one or more themes from 1984 with the young adult novel.
Persuasive Techniques _____ /20	Student uses at least three persuasive techniques that were learned in class. Each technique is effectively used to support argument.	Student uses two persuasive techniques that were learned in class. Both techniques are adequately used to support argument.	Student uses one or fewer persuasive techniques that were learned in class. Technique is not effectively used to support argument.
Publication _____ /10	Students follow requirements for formatting as presented on task cards. Product is professional in language and presentation. Few problems with spelling and grammar.	Students have minor problems following requirements for formatting as presented on task cards. Product is professional in language and presentation. Minor problems with spelling and grammar.	Students have major problems following requirements for formatting as presented on task cards. Product is unprofessional in language and presentation. Major problems with spelling and grammar.

SOURCE: Used with permission of Jessica Stopa and Julia Posey; TriMind Format from Doubet & Hockett, 2015.

C.4B   TRIMIND: ARITHMETIC AND GEOMETRIC SEQUENCES

Standards:

CCSS.MATH.CONTENT.HSF.BF.A.2

Write arithmetic and geometric sequences both recursively and with an explicit formula, use them to model situations, and translate between the two forms.

CCSS.MATH.CONTENT.HSF.IF.C.8

Write a function defined by an expression in different but equivalent forms to reveal and explain different properties of the function.

Understanding:

- Students will understand that patterns are evident in many areas in life (math).

Knowledge:

- The definition of a common difference.
- The definition of a common ratio.
- The definition of geometric sequence.
- The definition of arithmetic sequence.

Skills:

- Identify the common difference of arithmetic sequences.
- Identify the common ratio of geometric sequences.
- Extend arithmetic sequences.
- Extend geometric sequences.

Task Options (Choose One)		
Analytical	**Practical**	**Creative**
• Present a step-by-step approach to identifying common differences/ratios and extending arithmetic/geometric sequences to at least seven terms for your classmates. Include examples with your steps. • Include a defense of your approach that argues for is soundness • Make sure to define the types of sequences and the terms common difference and common ratio.	• Think of some times you have used arithmetic and geometric sequences in your everyday life. • Explain **how** you used these sequences and **why** it was helpful and important to use this process. • Make sure to define the sequence types, identify the common difference/ratio for your sequences and what these terms mean, and extend the sequences to at least seven terms.	• Create a new arithmetic and geometric sequence that extends to at least seven terms. • Come up with a context or story about where this sequence comes from or means. • Design a visual to clarify the terms in your sequence. • Make sure to define the types of sequences and common difference/ratio. Identify the common difference/ratio for your sequences.

Closure Activity

Students will be put together in a Jigsaw fashion to present their information (at least one student from each project category). This may take place at school or at home (via Google Hangout and Google Doc), depending on the flow of class. Students will then be given an exit ticket (again, at-school or at-home using TodaysMeet) that gives one arithmetic sequence and one geometric sequence. For each sequence, they will have to identify the common difference/ratio and extend the sequence by three terms.

Rubric

	3	2	1	0
Vocabulary	Included the four key definitions correctly: arithmetic/ geometric sequence and common difference/ratio.	Included three of the definitions correctly.	Included one or two of the definitions correctly.	Did not include any vocabulary.
Identifying Common Difference/Ratio	Identified the correct common difference and common ratio.	Identified only one of the two (common difference and common ratio) correctly.	Attempted but both common ratio and common difference are wrong.	Did not identify the common difference and common ratio— No attempt.
Extending Arithmetic/ Geometric Sequence	Extended both sequences correctly (right numbers) and to the correct number of terms.	Extended their sequences correctly but not to the correct number of terms.	Extended sequences to the correct number of terms but did not extend the sequences correctly (did not give the right numbers).	Did not extend their arithmetic and geometric sequence.

SOURCE: Used with permission of Heather Waller; TriMind Format from Doubet & Hockett, 2015.

Standard:

NGSS MS-ESS2-5

Collect data to provide evidence for how the motions and complex interactions of air masses result in changes in weather conditions.

Understanding:

- Students will understand that the Earth, a complex system, has many cycles (in this lesson, the hydrological cycle) that interact.

Knowledge:

- Weather is created by the transfer of energy between the Earth's surface and the atmosphere. (background knowledge—not directly assessed in this lesson)

- Convection, the transfer of heat from one thing to another, is a major cause of weather. (background knowledge—not directly assessed in this lesson)

- Weather is the day-to-day changes in atmospheric temperatures.

- Wind is created by unevenly distributed heat at Earth's surface combined with the spinning of Earth on its axis.

- An air mass is an extremely large body of air which can cover thousands of miles. These air masses can be polar (P) or tropical (T) and continental (c) or marine (m).

- A front is a transition between two air masses with different properties. Fronts are identified by a change in temperature, change in moisture in the air, shifting winds, pressure changes, and cloud and precipitation patterns.

- Different types of fronts include stationary, cold, warm, and occluded. Each of these fronts has characteristic weather that goes along with it.

- High pressure systems are generally related to nice weather, whereas low pressure systems are generally associated to poor weather.

- Cold air sinks; warm air rises. Air moves out of a high pressure system; air moves into a low pressure system. In a high pressure area (anticyclone), the air is sinking; in a low pressure area (cyclone), the air is rising.

- An isobar connects places of equal atmospheric pressure.

Skills:

- Describe the direction of local winds.

- Interpret a weather map containing high and low fronts, isobars, and pressure systems.

- Compare and contrast different weather maps/locations on the same weather map.

- Collect data to provide evidence for how the motions and complex interactions of air masses result in changes in weather conditions.

Task Options (Choose One)		
Analytical	Creative	Practical
Let's Take a Vacation!	**So You Want to Be a Meteorologist?**	**FIELD TRIP!!!!**
Given the two different weather maps provided by your teacher, compare and contrast the upcoming weather for people staying in your hometown for the holidays and people traveling to a beach vacation spot.	Imagine you are a meteorologist who is interviewing for a job at a local weather station in your hometown. Create a script suitable for local television weatherman, outlining the forecast for the upcoming weather for two different computer simulations (provided by your teacher).	You are preparing for the upcoming week at school. On Monday and Tuesday, you are at your regular school, but on Wednesday, you taking a field trip to a mountainous region (your teacher will provide you with two weather maps). Outline what differences there may be between the two locations (home and field trip location) and how you might prepare to accommodate the changes in weather.
Things to consider:	Interview Criteria:	
• Where is each parcel of air moving from? What type of front is at each location?	• What are the main differences between the two simulations? Are there different fronts? Is the air coming from different locations? What is the corresponding air pressure? Make sure you include the wind intensity and direction!	• What is the difference between the forecast for Monday and the forecast for Wednesday?
• What are the differences in air pressure between the two locations? What type of weather will occur at each other these locations?		• Where is the air coming from and what fronts are at each location? What is the difference in the air pressure systems?
• Based on the air pressure and the fronts, how windy will it be at the beach compared to at their home?	• Based on these items, what type of weather will the meteorologist have to prepare his audience for? Will his or her audience need to wear a windbreaker or a rain jacket or prepare for sunny skies?	• Will there be a change in weather between Monday and Wednesday?
• What direction will the wind blow?		• Will your field trip be rained out or will you only need to prepare for wind? Where is the wind coming from?
• Should the people traveling to the beach expect nice weather and how will the weather differ from their home?		

Closure Activity

The students will move into groups with one person from each task option and present what they accomplished for the task. The students will devise a list of important concepts that each of their projects contained. When all groups are finished, the class will create a master list of the key concepts in the activity by posting them to a Padlet board.

Rubric

	Clear Skies	Partly Cloudy	Drizzle
Collects data from and makes accurate comparison of the two weather maps	Identifies many (4+ for each) accurate similarities and differences between the two different weather models.	Identifies some accurate similarities and differences (1–3 each) between the two models.	Incorrect or missing similarities and differences of the two models.
Locates and understands what weather is associated with fronts	Correctly identifies the possible weather associated with the front.	Mostly correct identification of the possible weather associated with the front.	Scientifically invalid identification of the weather associated with the front.
	Provides a complete and correct explanation of why the type of weather is associated with the front.	Provides a partially complete and mostly correct explanation of why the type of weather is associated with the front.	Provides a scientifically invalid or incomplete explanation of why the weather is associated with the front.
Understands how air moves in relation to fronts	Complete, accurate, and thorough explanation of how air moves with fronts.	Partially incomplete and mostly correct explanation of how air moves with fronts.	Incomplete and incorrect explanation of how air moves with fronts.
Utilizes isobars to find air pressure	Correctly identifies the air pressure at different locations by utilizing isobars.	Identifies air pressure at one of the locations by using isobars.	Does not identify or incorrectly identifies air pressure.
Describes the direction and intensity of the wind	Based on the location of highs and lows, accurate and complete explanations of wind movement is provided.	Mostly complete and accurate explanations of wind movement based on the positions of highs and lows.	Incomplete or inaccurate explanations of wind movement based on highs and lows.
Methodology	Accurately followed the scientific method and the nature of science.	Generally accurate in following the scientific method and the nature of science.	Did not follow or made inaccurate use of the scientific method and nature of science.

SOURCE: Used with permission of Emily Chapin; TriMind Format from Doubet & Hockett, 2015.

C.4D TRIMIND: SOCIAL STUDIES

Standards:

Virginia SOL GOVT.6g

The student will demonstrate knowledge of local, state, and national elections by analyzing voter turnout.

CCSS.ELA-LITERACY.RH.6-8.1

Cite specific textual evidence to support analysis of primary and secondary sources.

Understandings:

- Students will understand that many people actively *choose* to not participate in the election process for various reasons.
- Students will understand that the percentage of voter turnout, and more specifically *who* turns up to vote, has a direct impact on election results.

Knowledge:

- Several possible causes of low voter turnout including age, gender, income, voter loyalty, voter apathy, current events/issues, competitiveness of the campaign, and chosen candidates, and so on.
- Voter turnout is affected by age, gender, and income.

Skills:

- Discuss several influencing factors on voter turnout in a given senate election.
- Conclude *how* various factors had a direct impact on voter turnout in a given senate election.
- Present a well-supported, reasoned, and organized case using evidence from primary and secondary sources.

Task Options (Choose One)		
Analytical	**Practical**	**Creative**
At Home: Take a look at the most recent senatorial election in Virginia.	**At Home:** Look at the most recent senatorial election in Virginia.	**At Home:** Research which senatorial election had the highest turnout and why
At School:	**At School:**	**At School:**
<ul><li>What was the voter turnout?</li><li>Make at least three different predictions about why it was at this level.</li><li>Explain what factors lead you to that conclusion.</li><li>Defend your conclusions with citations from articles</li></ul>	<ul><li>What was the voter turnout? What changes could have been made by either (or both) parties to increase this percentage?</li><li>Give at least three solutions and explain how this may have had an impact on the voter turnout. If you would like, you can also explain how you believe this may have affected the results of the election.</li></ul>	<ul><li>Imagine that voter turnout in the next Virginia senatorial election hit 100%. Create a scene for what would have led to this.</li><li>You may draw representations of what occurred, write about what occurred, create a news report about what occurred, or a combination.</li></ul>

(Continued)

(Continued)

and other resource information you find online. Predictions should be based on—and discuss—the various contributing factors discussed in class (and listed in knowledge goals).	Be sure to reference the contributing factors discussed in class (knowledge goals) in your explanation.	• You must have at least three separate aspects and explanations about how this happened. Be sure to reference the contributing factors discussed in class (and listed in knowledge goals) in your explanation.

Closure Activity

- First, students will be asked to match themselves with someone who chose a different task and discuss their responses. This will make students more comfortable sharing with the whole group later and may address misconceptions before whole class discussion. Hopefully, there will be one person from each task in a group, but this will ultimately depend on how many students chose each task.

- Then, the teacher will pull students back to whole group. Her or she will then ask students to share a factor they chose to use in their task and explain how they used it. Students should also explain why they chose that particular factor.

- Sticks of Accountability can be used to choose students at random, but at least one person from each activity should be chosen at some point.

- Depending on time, the teacher should ask *at least* three students to share (one from each task) and more if there is more time. Other students can chime in if the discussion sparks other ideas or questions.

- If there is a factor discussed that was incorrectly used, the teacher can ask the class how they might use that factor in a different way.

Rubric

Rubric Criteria (30 Points)			
You include at least three predictions/solutions based on the provided list of contributing factors as per your chosen role. (30%)	3	2	1
You include supportive evidence from reliable sources to back up your arguments/predictions/representations with reference to the contributing factors listed. (30%)	3	2	1
Your arguments/predictions/representations are logical and combine evidence with reasoning from sources and understanding of context. (30%)	3	2	1
Your finished product is easily read/understood and shows evidence of proofreading. (10%)	3	2	1

SOURCE: Used with permission of Amber Geary; TriMind Format from Doubet & Hockett, 2015.

....

Extended Management Example

In Chapter 4, we discussed how Graphic Organizers can be used to differentiate instruction for student readiness, but they can also help encourage student persistence, reflection, and investment in learning. Figures 6.5–6.7 from Chapter 6 on Management are again referenced below, this time illustrating teacher and student interactions more holistically using a social studies example on the origins of the Civil War. The first section describes the assignments students are completing, while Figure D.1 depicts a student's reflections and teacher feedback. The teacher and student can maintain this document (Figure D.1) confidentially on Google Drive (for more information about Google Drive, see Appendix A).

HIGH SCHOOL SOCIAL STUDIES–CIVIL WAR PRIMARY DOCUMENT ANALYSIS

Standard:

CCSS.ELA-LITERACY.RH.9-10.9

Compare and contrast treatments of the same topic in several primary and secondary sources.

Framing Question: Are conflicts inevitable?

Note: The graphic organizer in Figure D.1 should be filled in by students as they *progress through* this lesson.

FIGURE D.1: SOCIAL STUDIES GRAPHIC ORGANIZER FOR PERSISTENCE, REFLECTION, AND INVESTMENT

Origins of the Civil War Lesson

My Initial Response to the Framing Question	Teacher Feedback	How I Will Use This Feedback to Improve My Thinking
I've always been taught that conflicts can be avoided if both sides can compromise. So it's my belief that conflicts can be avoided with effective negotiating.	Your response shows that you have a good initial understanding of what conflicts are and how they can be avoided. However, there are some additional complexities in this lesson that will likely alter your thinking. I'm hoping that your surface-level understanding will progress to deeper levels!	I need to focus on how complex conflicts can be and consider revising my initial thinking based on this new information. I run into this problem a lot where I settle for the easy answer instead of going deeper. It's something I need to work on!

How Would I Rank My Effort on the Assignments for This Lesson? Provide one sentence why.

- Soaked in Perspiration
- Working Up A Good Sweat
- Slightly Perspiring
- Totally Dry

THE DIFFERENTIATED FLIPPED CLASSROOM

Introductory Framing Questions	Group Work Analyzing Primary Documents	At Home Video and Edmodo Response	Synthesis With Classmate Who Chose the Other Side
Totally Dry: I should have spent more time addressing the framing question from different angles. I answered the question more surface level instead of trying to go deeper.	Good Sweat: After the framing question, I knew I needed to invest more effort in my work, so I made it a point to contribute to the success of my group as a whole by highlighting key language to discuss. I think this paid off for the rest of the lesson.	Good Sweat: I loved the video and it really forced me to continue to rethink my conception of conflict and all the different components, both recent and earlier, that go into the decision to fight a war.	Soaked: I interacted well with my classmate (listened to her and spoke respectfully) and we came up with a really good synthesis on conflict and the Civil War—but it was tough! We kept going back and forth using our primary sources. My brain hurt after!

What Worked For Me In This Lesson	Why Do I Think This?	What Might Help My Learning Next Lesson?
The thing that worked best for me was the synthesizing activity where we worked with a partner. It was also where I invested the most effort. I guess that's the point huh??	I feel as though I work best in a very small group or with a partner. It can be overwhelming for me in a larger group and sometimes I don't put as much effort into it. Partners also help me get deeper with my thinking.	I like working with one other person, so I think that would be great. But I also know I need to get more complex ideas on my own. I think I did a good job with that this lesson, BUT I also know I need to be able to dig deeper into my ideas on my own.

At School: When students first enter the room, they are asked to reflect on the framing question (above) in their blogs, which are kept in LiveJournal (for more information about LiveJournal, see Appendix A). The teacher can use these reflections as a baseline to determine the progression of student thinking over the remainder of the unit. Once finished, students are invited to choose the perspective of either "The South" or "The North" for a primary document analysis. Once they have selected this initial perspective, students collaborate in small groups of three or four to analyze primary documents. For each group (North or South), there is one document arguing *for* going to war and one document arguing *against* it. Students must gather specific evidence from these sources and make an evaluative decision about whether or not the Civil War (conflict) could have been avoided from the perspective they have chosen (North or South). While students are working on this assignment, the teacher can look over the students' blog entries from the beginning of class and offer specific feedback on their responses by posting comments to their blogs.

At this point, the teacher has taken several steps to set an **inviting** tone in the classroom. First, students are asked to share their initial opinions to the framing question without judgment on the part of classmates or the teacher. Next, students are asked to select the perspective of either the North or the South to begin the assignment, harnessing the motivating power of choice, whether that choice is based on *interest* or even *readiness* (i.e., background knowledge of a particular side).

At Home: When students get home, they are asked to watch an excerpt from Ken Burns' Civil War documentary (https://www.youtube.com/watch?v= FN2huQB-DmE), and then edit their online journals (blogs) to supplement their initial response to the framing question: *Are conflicts inevitable?* Students conclude the assignment by responding to a poll on the class Edmodo site. The teacher uses this data to determine the percentage of students who felt the conflict could have been avoided versus the percentage who felt conflict was inevitable (for more information about Edmodo, see Appendix A).

At School: The following day in class, the teacher projects poll results from the night before to stimulate a brief discussion concerning the inevitability of conflict. Students then pair up with classmates who selected the other side of the conflict (i.e., someone who chose the North would partner with someone who selected the South) and attempt to reach consensus. In these groups, students share specific information gleaned from their primary source analysis. Students are asked to come back once more to their blog entries from the beginning of the lesson and reflect on how their thinking has changed. Last, students complete what is left of the Graphic Organizer in Figure D.1.

Student responses in this graphic organizer illustrate how teachers can lead their classroom in a way that allows each student to see himself or herself as a valuable, invited member of the class. It also depicts an atmosphere where expectations remain high regardless of student needs. Teachers should strive to create an environment where each student is expected to persist, reflect, and invest in his or her learning.

Differentiated Flipped Lesson Plan (FLP) Template and Sample Lessons

E.1 FLP TEMPLATE (DIFFERENTIATED FLIPPED LESSON PLAN)

Lesson Topic, Standards, and Learning Goals

Lesson Topic:

Standards:

Learning Goals:

Students will understand that

Students will know

Students will be able to

At-Home Learning Components to Include in Planning	At-School Learning Components to Include in Planning
Steps May Include:	Steps May Include:
• Content to Be Viewed • Active Processing • Meaningful Online Interactions With Peers or the Teacher • Formative Assessment to Check for Understanding • Summative Checks for Grasp of Content/Skills	• Activities Responding to, or Extending, At-Home Learning • Grouping/Meaningful Interactions With Peers or the Teacher • What Is Produced During Task(s) • Formative Assessment to Check for Understanding • Summative Checks for Grasp of Content/Skills

Steps of Lesson—Labeled With Components	Setting and Differentiation
Step 1:	Completed . . . ☐ At Home ☐ At School Differentiated? If so, how and why?
Step 2:	Completed . . . ☐ At Home ☐ At School Differentiated? If so, how and why?

THE DIFFERENTIATED FLIPPED CLASSROOM

Steps of Lesson—Labeled With Components	Setting and Differentiation
Step 3:	Completed . . . ☐ At Home ☐ At School Differentiated? If so, how and why?
Step 4:	Completed . . . ☐ At Home ☐ At School Differentiated? If so, how and why?
Step 5:	Completed . . . ☐ At Home ☐ At School Differentiated? If so, how and why?
Step 6:	Completed . . . ☐ At Home ☐ At School Differentiated? If so, how and why?
Step 7:	Completed . . . ☐ At Home ☐ At School Differentiated? If so, how and why?
Eventual Summative Assessment(s):	Completed . . . ☐ At Home ☐ At School Differentiated? If so, how and why?

Copyright © 2016 by Corwin. All rights reserved. Reprinted from *The Differentiated Flipped Classroom: A Practical Guide to Digital Learning* by Eric M. Carbaugh and Kristina J. Doubet. Thousand Oaks, CA: Corwin, www.corwin .com. Reproduction authorized only for the local school site or nonprofit organization that has purchased this book.

E.2 ELA FLP (DIFFERENTIATED FLIPPED LESSON PLAN)

Lesson Topic, Standards, and Learning Goals

Lesson Topic: Tenth Grade English—Showing Versus Telling in Creative Writing

Standards:

CCSS.ELA-LITERACY.W.9-10.3

Write narratives to develop real or imagined experiences of events using effective technique, well-chosen details, and well-structured event sequences.

CCSS.ELA-LITERACY.W.9-10.3.D

Use precise words and phrases, telling details, and sensory language to convey a vivid picture of the experiences, events, setting, and/or characters.

Learning Goals:

Students will understand that

- Images "shown" with description rather than "told" using explanation are more powerful for the reader.

Students will know

- The difference between showing and telling.
- The difference between explained descriptions and vivid images.
- The definitions and uses for many literary devices.

Students will be able to

- Portray vivid images in writing.
- Determine whether a passage is showing or telling.
- Interpret a situation in a showing passage using context clues.
- Develop a written piece that shows the situation rather than tells it.

At-Home Learning Components to Include in Planning	At-School Learning Components to Include in Planning
Steps May Include:	Steps May Include:
<ul><li>Content to Be Viewed</li><li>Active Processing</li><li>Meaningful Online Interactions With Peers or the Teacher</li><li>Formative Assessment to Check for Understanding</li><li>Summative Checks for Grasp of Content/Skills</li></ul>	<ul><li>Activities Responding to At-Home Learning</li><li>Grouping/Meaningful Interactions With Peers or the Teacher</li><li>What Is Produced During Task(s)</li><li>Formative Assessment to Check for Understanding</li><li>Summative Checks for Grasp of Content/Skills</li></ul>

Steps of Lesson—Labeled With Components	Setting and Differentiation
Step 1:	Completed . . .
Content to Be Viewed: Students watch the opening scene of Disney and Pixar's *Up* in which the entire background story is depicted without words. They are instructed to pay special attention to what is happening and how they know.	☒ At Home ☐ At School
https://www.youtube.com/watch?v=2PD7qi8VK_o	**Differentiated by Interest** to motivate students to complete the discussion post and to allow for the sharing of various perspectives.
Active Processing: After viewing the clip, students choose two of the three questions below to post on discussion board: • "What happened in this clip?" "They didn't speak, so how do we know?" • "Describe how the effect of the clip would have been different if the movie started with Carl standing up and saying 'I'm sad because I miss my wife.'" • "Brainstorm! How can we apply what is done in this clip (showing versus telling) to our own writing?"	
Step 2:	Completed . . .
Content to Be Viewed: Students watch a brief teacher-created lecture introducing showing versus telling in writing.	☒ At Home ☐ At School

• The video uses Captivate and includes excerpts from two versions of The Brothers Grimm's "Hansel and Gretel" (see links below)
 	
  1. A "showing" passage from the Gutenberg Project
 	
  2. A "telling" passage from speakaboos.com
 	
• The teacher presents definitions of "showing" and "telling" for the students to write in their notes.
 	
• The teacher then applies each definition to the "Hansel and Gretel" passages and explains why showing is more effective than telling, using highlighting within the text for emphasis.
 	
• Finally, the teacher "thinks aloud" while writing two more short passages to exemplify the showing technique.	

(Continued)

(Continued)

Steps of Lesson—Labeled With Components	Setting and Differentiation
Active Processing: While watching, students take notes on the definitions provided by the teacher and key examples from the lecture. They also record any questions they have or details that need clarity to post the next day (see Step 4). 	

	Definition	Key Example	Write Your Own Example
Showing			
Telling			
Questions About Showing Versus Telling:			

Steps of Lesson—Labeled With Components	Setting and Differentiation
Step 3: **Meaningful Interactions/Formative Assessment:** Students post two sentences on a Padlet board (padlet.com). One sentence will show and the other will tell. Both respond to the question "How do you feel when you watch your favorite movie?" • **Meaningful Interactions With Peers or the Teacher:** Because everyone can read the responses, students are able to respond to other answers and see examples if they are having trouble. • **Formative Assessment:** The teacher uses the answers to gauge understanding and drive instruction at school the following class period.	Completed . . . ☒ At Home ☐ At School
Step 4: **Activities Responding to At-Home Learning:** The teacher conducts a brief review of the difference between "showing" and "telling" in writing and answers any questions students pose based on the previous night's activities. **Meaningful Interactions With Peers or the Teacher/Formative Assessment:** Teacher pulls up the Padlet board from the night before on the screen. As a class, the students determine whether to move each sentence to one side or the other, sorting them into a "Show" column and a "Tell" column.	Completed . . . ☐ At Home ☒ At School

Steps of Lesson—Labeled With Components	Setting and Differentiation
Class discusses the differences between the two columns and together revises a few "telling" examples to make them "showing."	
Step 5: **Formative Assessment:** Students submit an online check-in in Google Forms. They include one "tell" sentence from the Padlet, rewritten into a "show" sentence and a ranking of their understanding 1 to 5. Teacher reviews these responses as students complete Step 6.	Completed . . . ☐ At Home ☒ At School
Step 6: **Activities Responding to At-Home Learning:** Students read the excerpt from O. Henry's *The Gift of the Magi* (http://www.corestandards .org/assets/Appendix_B.pdf, page 104) and highlight areas of the text that do a particularly powerful job of "showing" rather than "telling." They annotate their text explaining why they highlighted their selected portions.	Completed . . . ☐ At Home ☒ At School
Step 7: **Grouping:** Teacher splits the class into smaller groups of three to four students based on readiness as determined by their formative-assessment responses from the Google Form. **Meaningful Interactions With Peers or the Teacher/Product:** Students share their highlights and annotations of *The Gift of the Magi* and the teacher debriefs with students as a full class. Teacher gives each group a picture depicting a different scene. Each group composes eight sentences using vivid imagery that "shows" rather than "tells" what is going on in the scene. Teacher models one example for the class, and they come up with one sentence together. For example, for a picture is of someone building a sand castle, the modeled "show" sentence might be, "He carefully sculpted each tower with the edge of his shovel." **Differentiation:** • Students who "tell" rather than "show" and/or rate themselves low on understanding receive pictures of scenes already rich with details, actions, or	Completed . . . ☐ At Home ☒ At School Differentiated? If so, How and Why? **Differentiated by Readiness** to offer more scaffolding for those who need additional guidance and to challenge those with more developed understanding. (*Note:* By beginning the readiness portion with a shared activity—debriefing text highlights—less attention is drawn to the readiness grouping.)

(Continued)

(Continued)

Steps of Lesson—Labeled With Components	Setting and Differentiation
expressions (such as a pivotal moment in a sporting event or someone standing to make a speech with a painful expression on his face). • Those who "show" rather than "tell" and/or rate themselves high on understanding receive pictures of scenes that require more inferring or that are harder to describe (such as an empty field or a student simply standing at her locker). The teacher circulates throughout the room, checking in with each group. When everyone is done, the groups read their sentences to the class while someone from the other groups tries to draw the image on the board based solely on the descriptions.	

Step 8:
 	
 Formative Assessment: Exit slip: 3-2-1:
 	
 • Rewrite **3** telling sentences so that they show.
 	
   o *He ran screaming through the woods.*
 	
   o *He was really, really scared.*
 	
   o *The bear chased after him.*
 	
 • What are **2** things you could do to improve your own writing so that you show rather than tell?
 	
 • What is the **1** most pressing question you still have about showing versus telling in your own or other people's writing?
	Completed . . .
	
	 ☐ At Home
	
	 ☒ At School

Eventual Assessments: As part of the unit assessment, students will choose one of the following assignments.
 	
 • **Option 1** (Analytical): You are the editor of a credited newspaper (local or national). In reading this week's drafts, you notice that some of your writers are "telling" too much in their writing.
 	
   o Find a newspaper article that "tells" and write a letter to the writer explaining why he or she needs to edit the article.
 	
   o Highlight one part that "shows." Explain to the writer why this part is good.
	Completed . . .
	
	 ☒ At Home
	
	 ☒ At School
	
	 Differentiated? If so, How and Why?
	
	 Differentiated by Learning Profile according to TriMind (Sternberg's Triarchic Theory of Intelligence) for all students to display their understanding according to their choices/ strengths.

Steps of Lesson–Labeled With Components	Setting and Differentiation

o Choose another passage that "tells," and rewrite the passage so it "shows" to model good technique. Explain why you made these changes.
 	
• **Option 2** (Creative): Someone you know has asked you to write his or her biography. Write a sample chapter for the editor.
 	
    o Interview a friend or family member about a defining or exciting moment in his or her life. Remember to ask for specific details. (Alternative: Make up a person and event!)
 	
    o Use your writing to "show" us that event.
 	
• **Option 3** (Practical): What is a product you couldn't live without (favorite game, beauty product, etc.)? Write an Amazon review to "show" the product and its qualities/benefits. Your goal is for Amazon readers to rate it 5 stars for how useful it is.	

Lesson Resources: Hansel and Gretel (Step 2)

Hansel and Gretel by the Brothers Grimm via the Gutenberg Project

http://www.gutenberg.org/files/2591/2591-h/2591-h.htm#link2H_4_0020

Hansel and Gretel by the Brothers Grimm via Speakaboo

http://www.speakaboos.com/full-text/hansel-and-gretel

....

SOURCE: Used with permission of Gabrielle Munns.

E.3 MATH FLP (DIFFERENTIATED FLIPPED LESSON PLAN)

Lesson Topic, Standards, and Learning Goals

Lesson Topic:

Classifying relationships between quadrilaterals.

Standards:

CCSS MATH CONTENT 5.G.B.3

Understand that attributes belonging to a category of two-dimensional figures also belong to all subcategories of that category. For example, all rectangles have four right angles and squares are rectangles, so all squares have four right angles.

CCSS MATH CONTENT 5.G.B.4

Classify two-dimensional figures in a hierarchy based on properties.

Learning Goals:

Students will understand that

- Every quadrilateral in a subset has all the defining attributes of the subset

Students will know

- Quadrilaterals by descriptions of their different properties
- The terms quadrilateral, trapezoid, rectangle, rhombus, parallelogram, and square

Students will be able to

- Draw and define the properties of quadrilaterals
- Research and identify examples of real-life quadrilaterals
- Classify quadrilaterals based on their characteristics

At-Home Learning Components to Include in Planning	At-School Learning Components to Include in Planning
Steps May Include:	Steps May Include:
<ul><li>Content to Be Viewed</li><li>Active Processing</li><li>Meaningful Online Interactions With Peers or the Teacher</li><li>Formative Assessment to Check for Understanding</li><li>Summative Checks for Grasp of Content/Skills</li></ul>	<ul><li>Activities Responding to, or Extending, At-Home Learning</li><li>Grouping/Meaningful Interactions With Peers or the Teacher</li><li>What Is Produced During Task(s)</li><li>Formative Assessment to Check for Understanding</li><li>Summative Checks for Grasp of Content/Skills</li></ul>

Steps of Lesson—Labeled With Components	Setting and Differentiation
Step 1: **Active Processing/Content to Be Viewed:** Students are asked to watch the Socratica YouTube video and focus on what properties distinguish certain quadrilaterals from others. https://www.youtube.com/watch?v=CkbClyVxRIU Students are given the following instructions to complete while viewing the above video: ○ Copy the chart below in your notebook or on a loose-leaf paper. ○ Watch the video and fill in the middle column with a definition for each of the quadrilaterals. ○ Draw a rough sketch of the quadrilateral in the third column. (Don't worry if you do not feel confident drawing. Just try your best!)	Completed . . . ☒ At Home ☐ At School **Differentiated by Readiness:** Depending on the learning needs of the students, the teacher might add scaffolding to the graphic organizer in one or more of the following ways: 1. Provide the drawing. Example:

Quadrilateral	Definition	Drawing
Rhombus		
Rectangle		
Square		
Trapezoid		
Parallelogram		

Square	?	

2. Provide the definition and image and the student must correctly label the quadrilateral. Example:

?	4 congruent angles and side lengths	

3. Provide a worksheet in a language other than English.

Step 2: **Meaningful Interactions With Peers or the Teachers/Grouping/Active Processing/ Formative Assessment:** The following at-home blog post is given to students to complete after they have processed the video using the graphic organizer. The blogs can be viewed by the teacher and serve as a formative assessment.	Completed . . . ☒ At Home ☐ At School

(Continued)

(Continued)

Steps of Lesson—Labeled With Components	Setting and Differentiation

Students are provided with the following instructions:
 	
Go to your class blog on LiveJournal. You will need to make one post that includes both Section A and B below. Last, follow directions for Section C.
 	
Section A: Think of any school-appropriate object or item that is shaped like one of the quadrilaterals from the video. Search on Google to find an image of your quadrilateral-shaped object. Provide the following description for each image:
 	
   o *What is the object/item?*
   o *What quadrilateral shape is it?*
   o *What qualities define this type of quadrilateral?*
 	
Section B: Now think of a second object in the shape of a different quadrilateral from your first object. Make another Internet search for a school-appropriate image and post the IMAGE ONLY. One of your assigned group mates will describe the shape you chose (three students per group; each student has to describe one of their group mates' images).
 	
Section C: Reply to one of your classmates' posts and answer the following three questions for their second image:
 	
   o *What is the object/thing?*
   o *What quadrilateral shape is it?*
   o *What qualities define this type of quadrilateral?*
 	
(See an example of student blog on page 168.)	

Step 3: **Activities Responding to At-Home Learning:** The teacher begins class by leading a discussion to review the quadrilateral definitions from the at-home learning. The teacher provides students with the names of several quadrilaterals (square, rectangle, rhombus, parallelogram, and trapezoid) on the front board or projector. Next, the teacher distributes individual whiteboards and asks students to define and draw examples of these quadrilaterals on their whiteboards. The teacher should have students hold up their examples as an at school check for understanding before moving on to the next step.	Completed . . . ☐ At Home ☒ At School

Steps of Lesson–Labeled With Components	Setting and Differentiation
Step 4: **Activities Responding to At-Home Learning/ Grouping/Meaningful Interactions With Peers or the Teacher/Active Processing:** The teacher groups students based on prior misconceptions, errors, and understanding as demonstrated in the white-board formative assessment in Step 3. Groups should be about four to six students in size. The teacher provides each group with a set of quadrilaterals previously laminated and cut out by the instructor (see worksheet below). Have students create a "family tree" or "flowchart" by organizing the quadrilaterals based on their definitions. For example, a square should go below a rectangle because it has four congruent angles and two sets of parallel sides like the rectangle, but it also has four congruent sides. Students should be encouraged to explore the relationships between the shapes and should be able to justify the rationale for their quadrilateral family tree. (See example of quadrilateral concept map.) Students should list their classification criteria on paper next to their tree. After groups are finished organizing their quadrilaterals, have a member from each group explain to the entire class why they chose to put each quadrilateral where they did.	Completed . . . ☐ At Home ☒ At School **Differentiated by Readiness:** Examples of the quadrilateral concept map are provided to groups of students who need additional structure. These students showed errors or misconceptions on their work the night before or during the introductory activity (Step 4).
Step 5: **Formative Assessment:** To complete the lesson the teacher will gauge individual student understanding through an exit-card assessment. Students will respond to three statements by deciding if they think the statement is sometimes, always, or never true, and then briefly explain why they think that.	Completed . . . ☐ At Home ☒ At School

Statement	Sometimes	Always	Never	Why?
A rectangle is a square				
A square is a quadrilateral				
A rhombus is a parallelogram				

(Continued)

(Continued)

Steps of Lesson—Labeled With Components	Setting and Differentiation
Eventual Assessments: Learning Menu: Quadrilaterals Understandings for all courses: • Every quadrilateral in a subset has all the defining attributes of the subset Main Dish Knows: • Quadrilaterals by descriptions of their different properties • The terms quadrilateral, trapezoid, rectangle, rhombus, parallelogram, and square Main Dish Skills: • Draw and define the properties of quadrilaterals • Classify quadrilaterals based on their characteristics Side Dish Skills: • Identify examples of quadrilaterals in real-life settings Desserts will extend Main Dish Knows and Skills	Completed . . . ☐ At Home ☒ At School **Differentiated by Interest** to increase motivation—students may choose their tasks in the Side Dish and Dessert "courses."

Main Dishes: You must completing the following activities this week:
 	
1. Read through this webpage (www .mathisfun.com/quadrilaterals.html) and take notes on *each* quadrilateral.
 	
2. Complete the 10 "your turn" questions at the bottom of the "mathisfun" web page.
 	
3. Create a quadrilateral flipbook to include one page for each quadrilateral.
  o Drawing of each quadrilateral
  o Definition of its properties
  o 1 example
  o 1 nonexample with an explanation for why it is a nonexample
 	
4. Have at least one classmate peer review your quadrilateral flipbook AND peer review at least one other classmate's quadrilateral flipbook. A "peer review worksheet" must be filled out for each review.
 	
5. Make revisions to your flipbook based on the peer review of a classmate. Indicate what changes you made at the bottom of the peer-review worksheet of your flipbook. This worksheet will be turned in with your flipbook.	

Steps of Lesson—Labeled With Components	Setting and Differentiation
Side Dishes: Choose one option to complete during "menu time" next week: 1. On a classroom laptop, research two famous works of architecture (examples: One World Trade Center, St. Paul's Cathedral, Petronas Tower). Your goal is to find examples of the different quadrilateral shapes (square, rectangle, trapezoid, parallelogram, rhombus) in each of the buildings you select. Using www.pixlr.com you can draw over the images to highlight each of the quadrilateral shapes. Submit your work in *one* Google Doc when completed. 2. On a piece of paper (at *least* 8.5 x 11) make a drawing of something you see frequently in your community using ONLY quadrilateral shapes. Each quadrilateral shape must be easily identifiable in the drawing. You may draw anything after first confirming verbally or by e-mail with the teacher. Some examples: community basketball court, shopping center, the elementary school, and so on. 3. Bring in two digital photos of buildings in your neighborhood or around the school. Follow the same directions for Side Dish 1 to identify quadrilateral shapes for the pictures of your house and community building.	
Desserts (Complete as many as you have time to complete): 1. Comic: Create a comic strip using the quadrilateral shapes as main characters. The plot must include comparisons between the differences in shape between the characters. 2. School Quadrilateral Hunt: Take a journal to log notes with you and scavenge the school to find creative examples of each quadrilateral shape within the school. Make a note of where you found each shape and draw a brief sketch. (*Note:* Teachers can choose to limit the area that students may explore in to the classroom, the team hallway, or any other appropriate limitations; he or she can also send students on a photo scavenger hunt with an iPad instead of a journal.)	

(Continued)

Step 2 Blog Post Example

i. What is the object/thing?

....

Photo credit: © BananaStock/Thinkstock Photos

- Sticky notes

What quadrilateral shape is it?

- Square

What qualities define this type of quadrilateral?

- 4 congruent angles and 4 congruent sides.

ii. What is the object/thing?

....

Photo credit: © Spike Mafford/Thinkstock Photos

What quadrilateral shape is it?

What qualities define this type of quadrilateral?

....

SOURCE: Used with permission of Stephen Caviness.

E.4 SCIENCE FLP (DIFFERENTIATED FLIPPED LESSON PLAN)

Lesson Topic, Standards, and Learning Goals
Lesson Topic:
Modeling Genetic Probability with Punnett Squares
Standard:
Next Generation Science Standard MS-LS3-2 *Develop and use a model to describe why asexual reproduction results in offspring with identical genetic information and sexual reproduction results in offspring with genetic variation.*
Learning Goals:
Students will understand that • Genetic variation results from the cause and effect relationship of gene transmission from parent(s) to their offspring Students will know • Definitions of the terms allele, dominant, recessive, genotype, phenotype, and Punnett square Students will be able to • Predict the probability of theoretical genetic outcomes • Explain the process of genetic transfer from a unique perspective • Explain Gregor Mendel's pea-plant experiment as a model of genetic transfer

At-Home Learning Components to Include in Planning	At-School Learning Components to Include in Planning
Steps May Include: • Content to Be Viewed • Active Processing • Meaningful Online Interactions With Peers or the Teacher • Formative Assessment to Check for Understanding • Summative Checks for Grasp of Content/Skills	Steps May Include: • Activities Responding to, or Extending, At-Home Learning • Grouping/Meaningful Interactions With Peers or the Teacher • What Is Produced During Task(s) • Formative Assessment to Check for Understanding • Summative Checks for Grasp of Content/Skills

Steps of Lesson—Labeled With Components	Setting and Differentiation
Step 1: **Meaningful Online Interactions With Peers or the Teacher/Active Processing:** The entire class should first interact with one another through a backchannel created on Todaysmeet.com. In small groups of three to four, students engage in an approximately five-minute discussion concerning	Completed . . . ☒ At Home ☐ At School

(Continued)

(Continued)

Steps of Lesson—Labeled With Components	Setting and Differentiation
the essential question: "How can we predict which traits will pass down from one generation to the next?" AT MINIMUM, every student is expected to offer the following: 1. His or her meaningful reflection and thoughts; and 2. At least one response to each of the student's peers' comments.	
Step 2: **Content to Be Viewed/Formative Assessment/Active Processing:** 1. Students are asked watch the TedEd video at the following link: http://youtu .be/Mehz7tCxjSE 2. Students should read over the following two prompts and select the one they feel provides an appropriate level of challenge. They are asked post their individual responses to either Prompt 1 or Prompt 2 on their class blogs kept on Kidblog. This serves as the teacher's gauge for student understanding going into next day's class. *Note:* Students would not see the term "readiness," nor would they see the "level" information listed in the first column; rather, they would see only the standard and the prompts.	Completed . . . ☒ At Home ☐ At School **Differentiated by Readiness** through tiered prompts.

Readiness Prompt 1:

Standard:	
MS-LS3-2 *Develop and use a model to describe why asexual reproduction results in offspring with identical genetic information and sexual reproduction results in offspring with genetic variation.*	
One: Recall **(Who, What, When, Where, Why)**	What is the tool used to calculate the probability of an offspring's genotype called?
Two: Skill/Concept	What are all the possible genotypes for peas if Y = Yellow and y = green?
Three: Strategic Thinking	
Four: Extended Thinking	

Steps of Lesson—Labeled With Components	Setting and Differentiation
Readiness Prompt 2:	

Standard:

MS-LS3-2

Develop and use a model to describe why asexual reproduction results in offspring with identical genetic information and sexual reproduction results in offspring with genetic variation.

One: Recall **(Who, What, When, Where, Why)**	
Two: Skill/Concept	What are all the possible genotypes for peas if Y = Yellow and y = green?
Three: Strategic Thinking	Is there a possible way to crossbreed two pea plants and ensure 100% probability that they will produce only green pea plants? Use a Punnett square to show your thinking.
Four: Extended Thinking	

Steps of Lesson	Setting and Differentiation
Step 3: **Activities Responding to At-Home Learning/ Grouping/Meaningful Interactions With Peers or the Teacher:** At school, the teacher places students into pairs (with one group of three if there is an odd number). Students who self-selected a lower-readiness level are paired with students who self-selected the higher-readiness level. Have each pair of students read the short article at the following link: https://askabiologist.asu .edu/punnett-squares using available technology (or the teacher can print out hard copies ahead of time).	Completed . . . ☐ At Home ☒ At School

(Continued)

(Continued)

Steps of Lesson—Labeled With Components	Setting and Differentiation
After reading, each student is asked to complete the following chart (Steps 1–3) individually. When both have finished, they should discuss their answers with their partner to reach consensus, addressing any discrepancies that arise. 1. Copy and fill in the blanks in the following chart: 2. What is the probability of a green pea if two peas with genotypes AA and Aa are crossed? Create a Punnett square to check your answer. 3. What is the probability of a green pea if two peas with genotypes aa and Aa are crossed? Create a Punnett square to check your answer.	

Genotype	Phenotype
AA	
	yellow
	green

Steps of Lesson—Labeled With Components	Setting and Differentiation
Step 4: **Activity to Extend At-Home Learning:** Each student individually completes a RAFT, choosing from among the following prompts. Students can use any combination of Role, Audience, Format, and Topic (they do not have to follow a horizontal row across). Depending on the student's selection, products for this assignment may look very different; however, all students must meet the minimum requirements. RAFT—Mendel's Peas Minimum Requirements: • Include the terms Punnett square, dominant, and recessive. • Include details on how to use or read a Punnett square.	Completed . . . ☐ At Home ☒ At School **Differentiated by Interest** as students choose the RAFT option that is most appealing to them.

Steps of Lesson–Labeled With Components				Setting and Differentiation

Possible Roles	Possible Audiences	Choose a Format	Choose a Topic
Dominant/ Recessive Pea	Dominant/ Recessive Pea	Detailed Comic Strip	Explain alleles and dominance
News Anchor	Gregor Mendel	News Report	Discovery of genetic patterns
Teacher	Students	Class Activity	How to predict traits
Geneticist/ Doctor	New Mother/ Father	Script of Conversation	Explanation of genetic variability
Other	Other	Other	Mendel/ Inheritance/ etc.

Step 5:

Formative Assessment: To check for understanding, have each student respond to the following two questions on an index card.

1. Create a Punnett square to display the probability of genetic inheritance given the following genotypes and alleles.

   - B = brown eyes, b = blue eyes
   - Genotypes crossed: Bb and Bb

2. Consider the alleles for pea plants; yellow being dominant and green being recessive. Think of a trait that you possess.

   - What trait did you choose?
   - What is the dominant allele/form of that trait?
   - What is the recessive allele/form of that trait?

Completed . . .

☐ At Home

☒ At School

SOURCE: Used with permission of Stephen Caviness.

Lesson Topic, Standards, and Learning Goals

Lesson Topic:

Age of Exploration

Standards:

CCSS.ELA-LITERACY.RH.9-10.1

Cite specific textual evidence to support analysis of primary and secondary sources, attending to such features as the date and origin of the information.

CCSS.ELA-LITERACY.RH.9-10.2

Determine the central ideas or information of a primary or secondary source; provide an accurate summary of how key events or ideas develop over the course of the text.

Standard WHII.4a

The student will demonstrate knowledge of the impact of the European Age of Discovery and expansion into the Americas, Africa, and Asia by explaining the roles of explorers and conquistadors.

Learning Goals:

Students will understand that

- Humans explore and move for a variety of reasons
- Essential Question: Why do humans relocate?

Students will know

- The reasons for exploration
  o Demand for gold, spices, and natural resources in Europe
  o Expanding ship technology
  o Spread of Religion
  o Competition between European nations
- Main explorers
  o Portugal: Vasco da Gama
  o Spain: Christopher Columbus, Hernando Cortez, Ferdinand Magellan
  o England: Francis Drake
  o France: Jacques Cartier
  o Italy: Amerigo Vespucci

Students will be able to

- Analyze primary and secondary texts to find the primary reasons for exploration
- Use evidence from primary and secondary sources to create profiles of explorers

At-Home Learning Components to Include in Planning	At-School Learning Components to Include in Planning
Steps May Include: • Content to Be Viewed • Active Processing • Meaningful Online Interactions With Peers or the Teacher • Formative Assessment to Check for Understanding • Summative Checks for Grasp of Content/Skills	Steps May Include: • Activities Responding to, or Extending, At-Home Learning • Grouping/Meaningful Interactions With Peers or the Teacher • What Is Produced During Task(s) • Formative Assessment to Check for Understanding • Summative Checks for Grasp of Content/Skills

Steps of Lesson—Labeled With Components	Setting and Differentiation
Step 1: **Content to Be Viewed**: Students will view four 3-minute clips on the reasons for exploration and some of the main explorers: • https://www.youtube.com/watch?v=DtpuBsLHMd8 (Need for Trade Routes) • https://www.youtube.com/watch?v=1G7gVC7SUNs (Caravels) • https://www.youtube.com/watch?v=JplrfydOmQo (Voyage of Columbus) • https://www.youtube.com/watch?v=-VMj0d_hNW0 (Magellan) **Active Processing**: After watching the clips student will be asked to post the following on a discussion board: 1. Were Columbus and Magellan heroes or villains? Defend your answer with details from the clips and with your own reasoning. 2. Respond to a classmate's post that you disagree with raising a thought-provoking question to challenge their answer. Use details from the videos and/or your thinking to support your point, but use diplomatic language and a respectful tone.	Completed . . . ☒ At Home ☐ At School **Differentiated by Interest** (students choose a stance and argue for it) to motivate students to complete the discussion post and to allow for the sharing of various perspectives.
Step 2: **Activities Responding to At-Home Learning:** When students enter class they are asked to submit their favorite "Challenge" from the discussion board on a Padlet board (QR code provided). The teacher, in collaboration with students, will then organize/combine similar points together, and the class will discuss the implications of these points.	Completed . . . ☐ At Home ☒ At School

(Continued)

(Continued)

Steps of Lesson–Labeled With Components	Setting and Differentiation
Formative Assessment Check: The teacher then asks students to complete a Think/Pair/Share to discuss if the sacrifices of the explorers, their crews, their families, their countries, and those lands they explored "worth it." Teacher will use Class Dojo to call on volunteers to answer during the "share" phase.	
Step 3: **Grouping/Meaningful Interactions With Peers:** Next, the teacher asks students the framing question: "Why then, are people willing to relocate? What makes it 'worth it'? What would make it 'worth it' to you?" *Four Corners:* Students write the one place they want to move to if they could relocate anywhere and WHY. Students then place themselves in one of the four corners of the room based on the *reason behind their response* (e.g., if a student says he or she would move to Hawai'i, it might be because of aesthetics or because of an economic opportunity). Reasons for Relocating: • Altruism—To help those in need • Aesthetics—Beautiful place • Economics—Opportunity to make money • Expansion—Open space to build or grow The teacher then explains that these reasons are similar to those that prompted voyages during the age of explorers: missionary work, natural resources, gold and riches, and technology. In their corners, students discuss if and how their factor was influential to Columbus and/or Magellan (from videos). The teacher explains that other explorers were motivated by these factors and that students will determine just how much.	Completed . . . ☐ At Home ☒ At School **Differentiated by Interest** (Four Corners).
Step 4: **Grouping/Meaningful Interactions With Peers— JIGSAW:** Students select, based on interest, one explorer about whom they want to learn more. Names of explorers and their countries of origin will be displayed. Choices include • Portugal: Vasco da Gama • Italy: Amerigo Vespucci • Spain: Hernando Cortez • England: Francis Drake • England: John Cabot • France: Jacques Cartier	Completed . . . ☐ At Home ☒ At School **Differentiated by Interest** as students choose which explorer they will study for the jigsaw.

Steps of Lesson—Labeled With Components	Setting and Differentiation
Students then move into their expert groups based on the explorer of their choice and are provided with primary and secondary source documents on that explorer (via QR codes). Teacher monitors work during expert groups. After reading through the documents, students answer the following questions, recording their responses in a Google Doc to share with the other members of their home group. • What was the main factor for your explorer's journey, according to this document? • Was this factor/reason fulfilled? If yes, how? If no, why not? If yes OR no, what were the other results? • Was this a positive or a negative exploration? For whom? You must discuss multiple perspectives. • What implications did this exploration have for the world at large (both at the time of the voyage and in present day)? Home groups share information and code a map of North, Central, and South Americas, indicating which explorers influenced the development of which geographic areas.	**Differentiated by Readiness**: If reading levels or language proficiencies vary in the class, the teacher can provide different students with access to different websites via QR codes.
Step 5: **Formative Check for Understanding**: Individual students post their opinion of what factor (from Step 3)—on the whole—most heavily influenced the explorations they studied. Padlet results will be sorted and used to drive a classroom debate.	Completed . . . ☐ At Home ☒ At School
Step 6: **Meaningful Online Interactions With Peers/Final Check for Individual Understanding:** On www.kidblog.com, each student posts his or her final decision about the most important factor driving exploration. Students must support their opinion with evidence from at least three explorers other than those they studied in their expert groups. Students are also required to give one "glow" to the reasoning of a classmate who posted an opinion different from theirs.	Completed . . . ☒ At Home ☐ At School **Differentiated by Interest** as students can discuss their personal opinions.

SOURCE: Developed with Morgan Braun. Used with permission.

References

Anderson, L. W., Krathwohl, D. R., Airasian, P. W., Cruikshank, K. A., Mayer, R.E., Pintrich, P. R., . . . Wittrock, M. C. (2000). *A taxonomy for learning, teaching, and assessing: A revision of Bloom's Taxonomy of Educational Objectives.* New York, NY: Pearson, Allyn & Bacon.

Aronson, E., & Patnoe, S. (1997). *The jigsaw classroom: Building cooperation in the classroom* (2nd ed.). New York, NY: Longman.

Basye, D. (2014, August 5). *Personalized vs. differentiated vs. individualized learning.* Retrieved from https://www.iste.org/explore/articledetail?articleid=124

Bergmann, J. (2013). *Key questions you should ask before you flip your classroom.* Retrieved from http://flipped-learning.com/?p=1268

Bergmann, J., & Sams, A. (2012). *Flip your classroom: Reach every student in every class every day.* Alexandria, VA: ASCD.

Blackwell, L. S., Trzesniewski, K. H., & Dweck, C. S. (2007). Implicit theories of intelligence predict achievement across and adolescent transition: A longitudinal study and an intervention. *Child Development, 78*(1), 245–263.

Bransford, J. D., Brown, A. L., & Cocking, R. R. (Eds.). (2000). *How people learn: Brain, mind, experience, and school.* Washington, DC: National Academy Press.

Buehl, D. (2009). *Classroom strategies for interactive learning* (3rd ed.). Newark, DE: International Reading Association.

Burke, J. (2002). *Tools for thought: Helping all students read, write, speak, and think.* Portsmouth, NH: Heinemann.

Carbaugh, E. M. (2014). Designing reliable and valid math CCSS aligned assessments. *ASCD Express, 9*(12).

Chabris, C., & Simons, D. (1999). Gorillas in our midst: Sustained inattentional blindness for dynamic events. *Perception, 28*(9), 1059–1074.

Cooper, H., Robinson, J. C., & Patall, E. A. (2006). Does homework improve academic achievement? A synthesis of research, 1987–2003. *Review of Educational Research, 76,* 1–62.

Csikszentmihalyi, M. (1990). *Flow: The psychology of optimal experience.* New York, NY: Harper & Row.

Cummings, C. (2000). *Winning strategies for classroom management.* Alexandria, VA: ASCD.

Dean, C. B., Hubbell, E. R., Pitler, H., & Stone, B. (2012). *Classroom instruction that works: Research-based strategies for increasing student achievement* (2nd ed.). Alexandria, VA: ASCD.

Doubet, K. J. (2007). Teacher fidelity and student response to a model of differentiation as implemented by one high school (Doctoral dissertation). University of Virginia, Charlottesville.

Doubet, K. J., & Hockett, J. A. (2015). *Differentiation in middle and high school: Strategies to engage all learners.* Alexandria, VA: ASCD.

Duckworth, A. L. (2013, April). *The key to success? Grit* [Video]. Retrieved from http://www.ted.com/talks/angela_lee_duckworth_the_key_to_success_grit?language=en

Dweck, C. (2006). *Mindset: The new psychology of success.* New York, NY: Random House.

Dweck, C. (2007). The perils and promises of praise. *Educational Leadership, 65*(2), 34–39.

Emmer, E. T., Evertson, C. M., & Worsham, M. E. (2003). *Classroom management for secondary teachers* (6th ed.). Boston, MA: Allyn & Bacon.

Fisher, D., & Frey, N. (2012). Making time for feedback. *Educational Leadership, 70*(1), 42–47.

Fisher, D., & Frey, N. (2013). *Better learning through structured teaching: A framework for the gradual release of responsibility* (2nd ed.). Alexandria, VA: ASCD.

Frayer, D., Frederick, W. C., & Klausmeier, H. J. (1969). *A schema for testing the level of cognitive mastery.* Madison: Wisconsin Center for Education Research.

Gardner, H. (1995). Reflections on multiple intelligences: Myths and messages. *Phi Delta Kappan, 77,* 200–209.

Gardner, H. (2006). *Multiple intelligences: New horizons in theory and practice* (Rev. ed.). New York, NY: Basic Books.

Grant, P., & Basye, D. (2014). *Personalized learning: A guide for engaging students with technology.* Eugene, OR: International Society for Technology in Education.

Harrisonburg City Public Schools. (n.d.). *Guidelines for the use of student-owned technological devices.* Retrieved from http://web.harrisonburg.k12.va.us/tech/docs/tech_plan/Guidelines_Student_Devices.pdf

Hattie, J. (2012). *Visible learning for teachers: Maximizing impact on learning.* New York, NY: Routledge.

Hattie, J., & Yates, G. (2014). *Visible learning and the science of how we learn.* Thousand Oaks, CA: Corwin.

Jensen, E. (2005). *Teaching with the brain in mind* (2nd ed.). Alexandria, VA: ASCD.

Kagan, S., & Kagan, M. (2009). *Kagan cooperative learning.* San Clemente, CA: Kagan.

Lemov, D. (2010). *Teach like a champion: 49 techniques that put students on the path to college.* San Francisco, CA: Jossey-Bass.

Marzano, R. J. (2007). *The art and science of teaching: A comprehensive framework for effective instruction.* Alexandria, VA: ASCD.

Marzano, R. J., Marzano, J. S., & Pickering, D. J. (2003). *Classroom management that works: Research-based strategies for every teacher.* Alexandria, VA: ASCD.

Marzano, R. J., Pickering, D. J., & Pollock, J. E. (2001). *Classroom instruction that works: Research-based strategies for increasing student achievement.* Alexandria, VA: ASCD.

National Institute of Health. (2005). *The brain: Our sense of self.* Retrieved from http://science.education.nih.gov/supplements/nih4/Self/default.htm

O'Connor, K. (2011). *A repair kit for grades* (2nd ed.). Boston, MA: Pearson.

Organisation for Economic Co-operation and Development. (2012). *PISA 2012 Results in focus: What 15-year olds know and what they can do with what they know.* Paris, France: OECD.

Perry, B. D. (2000). How the brain learns best. *Instructor, 110*(4), 34–35.

Project Tomorrow. (2013). *From chalkboards to tablets: The emergence of the K–12 digital learner.* Speak up 2012 national findings. Retrieved from http://tomorrow.org/speakup/pdfs/SU12-Students.pdf

Salaway, G., Caruso, J. B., & Nelson, M. R. (2007). *The ECAR Study of undergraduate students and information technology, 2007.* Retrieved from http://www.educause.edu/ir/library/pdf/ers0706/rs/ERS0706w.pdf

Santa, C. (1988). *Content reading including study systems: Reading, writing and studying across the curriculum.* Dubuque, IA: Kendall Hunt.

Schraw, G., Flowerday, T., & Lehman, S. (2001). Increasing situational interest in the classroom. *Educational Psychology Review, 13*(3), 211–224.

Singer, N. (2015, January 11). Silicon Valley turns its eye to education. *The New York Times.* Retrieved from http://www.nytimes.com/2015/01/12/technology/silicon-valley-turns-its-eye-to-education.html?_r=0

Sousa, D. A., & Tomlinson, C. A. (2011). *Differentiation and the brain: How neuroscience supports the learner-friendly classroom.* Bloomington, IN: Solution Tree Press.

Sternberg, R. J., & Grigorenko, E. L. (2007). *Teaching for successful intelligence* (2nd ed.). Thousand Oaks, CA: Corwin.

Stiggins, R., & Chappuis, J. (2005). Using student-involved classroom assessment to close achievement gaps. *Theory into Practice, 44,* 11–18.

Stiggins, R., & Chappuis, J. (2012). *An introduction to student-involved assessment for learning* (6th ed.). Boston, MA: Pearson.

Strickland, C. A. (2007). *Tools for high-quality differentiated instruction: An ASCD action tool.* Alexandria, VA: ASCD.

Tomlinson, C. A. (2003). *Fulfilling the promise of the differentiated classroom.* Alexandria, VA: ASCD.

Tomlinson, C. A. (2005, July). *Keynote presentation: Differentiating instruction to meet the needs of all learners.* Presented at the Institutes on Academic Diversity: Summer Institute on Academic Diversity. Charlottesville, VA.

Tomlinson, C. A. (2014). *The differentiated classroom: Responding to the needs of all learners* (2nd ed.). Alexandria, VA: ASCD.

Tomlinson, C. A., & Doubet, K. J. (2005). Reach them to teach them. *Educational Leadership, 62*(7), 8–15.

Tomlinson, C. A., & Imbeau, M. B. (2010). *Leading and managing a differentiated classroom.* Alexandria, VA: ASCD.

Walkington, C. A. (2013). Using adaptive learning technologies to personalize instruction: The impact of relevant contexts on performance and learning outcomes. *Journal of Educational Psychology, 105*(4), 932–945.

Webb, N. (2002, March 28). *Depth of knowledge levels for four content areas.* Unpublished manuscript, Wisconsin Center for Educational Research.

Wiggins, G. (2012). Seven keys to effective feedback. *Educational Leadership, 70*(1), 10–16.

Wiliam, D. (2012). Feedback: Part of a system. *Educational Leadership, 70*(1), 30–34.

Willingham, D. T. (2003/2004). Why students think they understand—When they don't. *American Educator, 27*(4), 38–48.

Willis, J. (2006). *Research-based strategies to ignite student learning.* Alexandria, VA: ASCD.

Willis, J. (2007). The neuroscience of joyful education. *Educational Leadership, 64*(9). Retrieved from http://www.ascd.org/publications/educational-leadership/summer07/vol64/num09/The-Neuroscience-of-Joyful-Education.aspx

Willis, J. (2011). *A neurologist makes the case for the video game model as a learning tool.* Retrieved from http://www.edutopia.org/blog/video-games-learning-student-engagement-judy-willis#comments

Yarbro, J., Arfstrom, K. M., McKnight, K., & McKnight, P. (2014). *Extension of a review of Flipped Learning* (literature review). Washington, DC: Pearson and the Flipped Learning Network. Retrieved from http://researchnetwork.pearson.com/wp-content/uploads/613_A023_FlippedLearning_2014_JUNE_SinglePage_f.pdf See more at: http://researchnetwork.pearson.com/library#sthash.QUN2eTIF.dpuf

Index

CORWIN

A SAGE Company

Helping educators make the greatest impact

CORWIN HAS ONE MISSION: to enhance education through intentional professional learning.

We build long-term relationships with our authors, educators, clients, and associations who partner with us to develop and continuously improve the best evidence-based practices that establish and support lifelong learning.

Solutions you want. Experts you trust. Results you need.

Author Consulting
Author Consulting

On-site professional learning with sustainable results! Let us help you design a professional learning plan to meet the unique needs of your school or district. www.corwin.com/pd

Institutes
Institutes

Corwin Institutes provide collaborative learning experiences that equip your team with tools and action plans ready for immediate implementation. www.corwin.com/institutes

eCourses
eCourses

Practical, flexible online professional learning designed to let you go at your own pace. www.corwin.com/ecourses

Read2Earn
Read2Earn

Did you know you can earn graduate credit for reading this book? Find out how: www.corwin.com/read2earn

Contact an account manager at (800) 831-6640 or visit **www.corwin.com** for more information.